THE BITS _and_ PIECES THAT MAKE ME

A Campaigner for Secular Humanism

CHRISTOPHER C. BELL JR., ED.D.

_a.k.a._

KWAZI ANKOANNA ASANTE

Brilliant Books Literary
137 Forest Park Lane Thomasville
North Carolina 27360 USA

DEDICATION

This book is dedicated to all the people: who made me inquisitive enough to ask questions that others may have thought about asking, but never did; who engaged me in discussions that forced me to think; and who extended their personal comfort zones to embrace me as a friend even when we differed in our thinking on things spiritual as well as physical.

PROLOGUE

WHY I WROTE THIS AUTOBIOGRAPHY

I say that I am a humanist. What is a humanist? There are several definitions of a humanist, but they all coalesce around the following definition; a humanist is a person who believes in a system of values and practices based on the idea that human problems can best be solved by using reasoning instead of religion. A humanist is a person who attempts to adhere to the following commitments, beliefs, and affirmations:

COMMITED TO:

- **Applying reason and science to the understanding of the universe and to solving human problems, not religion;**

- **The principle of the separation of religion and government;**

- **The free and responsible search for truth and meaning;**

- **Promoting human empathy, compassion, and love;**

- **Working to secure justice and fairness in society, and eliminating racial discrimination and intolerances.**

BELIEVING THAT:

- **Every person is endowed with inherent worth and dignity and is deserving of human rights;**

- **An open, pluralistic, democratic society based on laws, equal justice, and due process, is the best way to protect human rights;**

- **We should cultivate moral and civic excellence such as altruism, integrity, honesty, justice, equity, and compassion in human relations;**

AFFIRMING WITH WORDS AND ACTIONS:

- **That humanism is a philosophy of living that is a realistic alternative to theologies of despair, fear, heavenly promises, and ideologies of violence;**
- **That humanism is a moral way for acquiring personal satisfaction and providing service to others.**

> **Note:** A portion of this listing of values was excerpted from "Affirmations of Humanism: a statement of principles." (Free Inquiry Magazine, Dec 2004).

As a campaigning humanist, I work to inform others that to improve the quality of our lives and to change America's culture toward a more authentic democratic ethos of law, justice, and respect for human rights, we must rely on human values and efforts rather than on so-called supernatural or divine (God) powers.

Why did I write this autobiography? I wrote this autobiography to describe for posterity, for my family, and for the reading public some of the bits and pieces of my life experiences that have made me a campaigning humanist, with the hope that they might learn something about themselves that will allow them to live happier and more fruitful lives.

I also wrote this book as a forward step in my campaign for humanism and my struggle to stop the "Jesus worshipping" practices/protocol of many black or non-white Christians. My reasoning and intuition tell me that Jesus worshipping is "white male worshipping," and that such worship practices are psychologically, socially, and emotionally deleterious to non-white people. My "campaigning efforts" consist of aggressively teaching and writing in order to:

a) explain to all Christians, black and white, that they should stop their Jesus worshipping (not Jesus following) practices wherein they bow down to worship the likeness (image) of a white male as the Savior of the world or the Son of God, because such a worship protocol promotes racism in white people and psychological self-oppression and self-denigration in non-white people; and,

b) encourage all people to adopt humanistic values in modeling their philosophies of life.

I wrote this book to experience the mental and emotional therapy that might be involved in the remembering, the thinking, the re-thinking, the self-analysis, and the self-discipline that writing such a book would require. As a young man, I knew very little about the life changing and directing forces that would shape my character, my spirituality, and ultimately my destiny. In the writing of this book, I am now aware of the alternative routes my life might have taken that would have made me a different person than I am today. In retrospect, I realize that I am not much better than most of the bad people I've met and that I am not much worse than most of the good people I've met; I am just luckier than some of them. And this realization makes me profoundly grateful for life and soberly aware of its fragility and unpredictability.

And finally, I wrote this book with the hope that its contents will become food for thought for those who chance to read it.

Christopher C. Bell Jr. Ed.D.
Aka
Kwasi Ankoanna Asante

CONTENTS

1.0 THE LAY OF THE MAN, THE LAND, AND THE TIMES

1.10 THE LAY OF THE MAN:

I was born May 7, 1933, a Sunday, at 1124 Covel Street in Campostella, a small, poor Negro suburb of Norfolk, Virginia.

I am 80 years old at the beginning of this writing and still in my right mind; although some might doubt it;

I am grateful for this incredible blessing (and mystery) of consciousness which we call "life";

I am in part the result of my experiences and my interactions with many people; some of whom treated me well and some of whom treated me otherwise;

I am in part the bits and pieces of the lessons learned and remembered from the suggestions, applause, criticisms, and teachings of many people;

I am still in the process of developing and hopefully becoming a better person as I continue to react to every-day situations that fate and chance bring my way.

1.11 MY ANCESTRY/GENES:

I am the great, grandson of American Negro slaves. I presume that all my people came to America from the coast of West Africa, but I don't really know. Once upon a time, I began to research the history of my forefathers. My research efforts took me back to the years 1836 and 1850 respectively of the Williams and the Bell families. I became depressed as I began to imagine the "slave days" of my American ancestors and I said "To hell with it" and stopped my research. I passed my research notes to younger family members so that they might continue the research if they desired. I now simply acknowledge my American slave ancestry and move on.

My Dad's parents migrated from North Carolina to Norfolk, Virginia, but I don't know from where or the year of that migration. My mother's parents migrated from Roanoke, Alabama to Norfolk, Virginia in 1916.

My mother, Olivia Williams, whom I called "mama," and my father, Christopher C. Bell, whom I called "daddy," met and married in Norfolk, Virginia (date unknown); and there, I was born and raised.

1.20 THE LAY OF THE LAND:

I grew up in the Negro section of Campostella, a rural, poor section of the south-side of Norfolk, Virginia. Rigid racial segregation was the prevailing, unquestioned ethos and practice of the day during my youth. Black families lived from paycheck to paycheck or from hustle to hustle. The navy or the shipyard related businesses were the sources of much of the employment. Campostella itself was a backwash or poor hind-side, section of Norfolk, Virginia.

> **Note: How Campostella got its name:** During the Civil War, there was a southern military out-post on the south side of the Elizabeth River in Norfolk, Virginia. The outpost commander had a daughter whose name was Stella. Since his outpost was without a name, the commander began referring to the camp as "Camp Stella." In the typical diction and dialect of the time, Camp-Stella began to ring out as Campo-stella, and that's what this small area of Norfolk is called today. (This information comes from the research of Dr. Melvin O. Smith; (Campostella Reunion Pamphlet, 1988, unpublished)

1.30 THE TIME OF THE TIMES

1.31 AMERICA; THE GRAND, FREEDOM-WAVING HYPOCRITE:

a) In 1933, the year I was born, America was the greatest hypocrite among the nations of the world with regards to its popular slogan and its vocal commitment to freedom, liberty, equality, and the fair treatment for all its citizens. Perhaps America's hypocrisy showed because it had made a declaration of freedom and liberty for all its citizens while the other nations of the world minority population the same way but they had not brandished a motto of freedom and liberty for all their citizens as America had done. In any event, as a black baby born in America in 1933, I and all black people were at the bottom of the bottom of the social order, except for the Native Americans. America was intensely apartheid. Most states had adopted laws called "Jim Crow laws." These laws granted to white citizens many privileges that were not granted to black citizens.

b) In 1931, 1932, and 1933, in America, there were over 60 lynchings of black men by white men, and the President of the United States and the Congress of the United States ignored the appeal of black leaders for the passage of federal anti-lynching laws.

c) In 1933, Adolph Hitler of Germany had just come to power and this event fore-shadowed the oncoming of World War II.

d) In 1933, European Christian nations were firmly entrenched in Africa, India, and southeast Asia as colonial occupiers and were dedicated to spreading their Christian concepts of God, extracting gold, minerals, and natural resources from these countries, and promoting their national self-glorification and self-interest under the label of civilizing the undeveloped, semi-savage, third world nations.

e) In 1933, the American economy was experiencing the greatest depression of its history and many people, blacks and whites, were stricken with poverty and unemployment.

f) In 1933, white supremacy was the unquestioned cultural doctrine that pervaded America and most of the civilized world. White supremacy served as a basic tenet of most European exploration and colonialism, and in America, it defined itself with its Jim Crow Laws that formed the relationship between white people and non-whites.

g) In 1933, the American Indian (Native Americans) had been on reservations for over 50 years and had been virtually forgotten by other Americans.

h) In 1933, America was viewed by most of the world as the grand promise-land of human freedom, liberty, and prosperity.

1.32 CAMPOSTELLA FROM A BLACK SOCIAL PERSPECTIVE:

From the 1930s thru the 1950s, Campostella was an outlying suburb of Norfolk, Virginia of mostly single family wooden houses, except for the two or three brick houses lived in by doctors or undertakers. Campostella was surrounded by the woods of Tarapin Hill, the Berkley (Norfolk and Western) railroad and the white neighborhoods of Newton Park and South Norfolk. I lived in a very rural part of Campostella where there were lots of fields, and no public water or electricity until I was about 9 years old.

What I remember about the adult social register in descending order is as follows:

a) One doctor, Dr. Green (who looked white enough to pass);

b) Preachers, at least two, perhaps three; two undertakers (Pretlows and Gordon);

c) Teachers (Mrs. Skinner and Miss Ross), practical nurses and mid-wives;

d) Grocery store and convenient store owners (Clark's and Jenkins' Stores on Wilson Rd, and Sharpe's Groceries located two blocks from our house on Pike Street. At Sharpe's store, I remember the large 5 cent candy-bars and bottles of pop (soda). I also remember the hard-candy jaw-breakers and the tootsie rolls and lollipops that sold for a penny);

e) Postmen (Mail carriers) about 7 (including my father)

f) Shipyard workers and craftsmen;

g) Entrepreneurs, journeymen, farmers, carpenters, longshoremen, and day laborers;

1.33 Campostella from an Economic Perspective:

In 1933, Norfolk was a mid-size, racially segregated city, but it offered more economic opportunities for black people than most American southern cities. Norfolk was a big-time economic-military employment-engine compared to many small, rural, back-wood or agricultural towns of America's south. During the years 1938-1950, Norfolk with its many governmental, military-industrial facilities showed itself as a genteel, white racist, segregationist culture with a cosmopolitan flavoring. In Campostella there were only a few small black businesses; the Welch Clark's grocery store, the Gordon Funeral Home, the Sharpe's corner store, several confectionaries, one black doctor, and two honky-tonks (that sold beer). The people living in Campostella had to go across the railroad tracks to Berkley, another black community, to the find a black owned pharmacy/drug store (owned by Dr. Wells).

Jewish families owned the major businesses in the Campostella and Berkley neighborhoods on which blacks were dependent. Their businesses were mostly located in Berkley and included a movie theater, a large eatery and beer garden, a Five and Dime store, housing and apartment buildings, a furniture store, and a pawn (loan) and cash-checking store.

The black people living in Campostella were poor, including my family, but I didn't realize this fact until I was in high school where I had an opportunity to compare my childhood situation to that of my classmates.

1.34 CAMPOSTELLA WAS BLESSED BY THE SOCIETAL TURBULENCE OF WORLD WAR II:

World War II gave Norfolk and Campostella an economic boom. During the war years, the city of Norfolk and the federal government began upgrading Campostella to accommodate the influx of black people who were relocating to Norfolk to work in military-support establishments. This upgrading included the building of the large apartment complexes of Anderson Park and Oak-leaf Park, a new (R.A. Tucker) elementary school, street paving, and installing electricity and digging sewage lines in Campostella.

Many, if not most black men worked in military-support establishments. My guess is that America's preparation for World War II and the war itself changed America's race-relations for the better and changed it in ways that would not have been possible if World War II had not taken place. Because of the war, many different people and foreigners came to Norfolk to work and Norfolk's environs became cosmopolitan as compared to many other southern cities. With the war came large numbers of people, the building of better schools, and a better public transportation system. Norfolk was transformed from a rigidly, racially segregated, small-town city to a hustling, bustling, big-town that was not so rigidly segregated.

As I look back now, I feel that had it not been for World War II and the fact that I lived in Norfolk, Virginia, and not in an agricultural or mining area of Virginia or in another southern state, that I would have become a different type of man than the man I am today. I don't know how much different I would be, but I don't think I would believe in myself as I do now, nor would I have the same outlook on life or the same character flaws or strengths. This realization on my part adds to the thoughtfulness of the question: "Do great times make great men or do great men make great time?"

2.0 Early childhood remembrances

2.10 EARLIEST PRE-SCHOOL MEMORIES:

2.11 AS A BABE,

I remember being carried in somebody's arms and smelling wet grass and seeing a faded rainbow partially covered by dark clouds, and at the same time I saw a part of the sky looking like a reddish sunset or sunrise.

2.12 AS A PRESCHOOLER (3-5 YEARS OLD),

We (Daddy, Mama, and my oldest sister Madeline and I) lived in a small house on the Campostella side of the Norfolk and Western railroad about 75 yards from where the railroad crossed Berkley Avenue. This house and the fields surrounding it were replaced long ago by a lumber mill establishment, but I remember the following things at that location:

a) We had a milk cow in our yard.

b) Our house would shake when trains would rumble pass.

c) My oldest sister, Madeline, and I would sometimes lie on our backs on the back porch and watch puffy white clouds slowly changing shapes as we tried to make the clouds into familiar figures.

d) One day Madeline and I saw Daddy about 2 blocks away as he was coming home (toward us). He was coming from work and we raced to meet him. His clothes were muddy and covered with dirt and he carried a bucket in one hand. Daddy put the bucket down and hugged us, and we walked with him to the house. Madeline held his one free hand and I walked ahead. He had a turtle in the bucket. Later, maybe the next day, Mama made us turtle soup.

e) Sometimes Madeline and I would stand at the edge of Berkeley Avenue and watch trains pass our house. Sometimes trains were made up of lots of railcars filled with coal and passed slowly. When that happened, long lines of cars and a few horse-drawn wagons formed and waited on each side of the railroad tracks for the train to clear the road crossing.

f) Early one summer night, Mama called to me to come out on the porch to see a big, orange-colored moon coming up from behind the trees in the Campostella eastern sky. It was the biggest moon ever.

g) Sometimes Madeline and I would walk out of the yard and go close to the railroad tracks and wave to the people who looked out the windows of the fast moving, rumbling passenger trains. Sometimes the people would wave back.

2.20 EARLY MEMORIES FROM 1121 PIKE STREET:

I don't remember when, but our family moved from the small house near the railroad tracks into another small house that I later came to know as 1121 Pike Street. This house was located in the "Over the field" area of Campostella. The area was very rural with many fields and open spaces; that why it was called "Over the field."

2.21 WE WERE POOR:

a) Dad planted and harvested vegetables. We raised chickens, geese, and ducks. We had no indoor running water. We had an indoor water pump and used kerosene lamps at night. We finally got electricity when I was 9 or 10 years old.

b) Up until I was 12-13 years old, we used a galvanized tin-tube for Saturday night baths. We used an out-house (toilet) located in our backyard about 30 yards from our house.

c) I remember several days when Mama Olivia put cardboard in the bottom of my shoes because we couldn't afford to buy new shoes for me. I just put the cardboard in my shoes and thought no more about it. As I look back now, I understand how poor we all were. But when World War II began things changed. The war brought work opportunities.

d) I remember that Grandma and Grandpa Bell received some type of welfare support. I also remember that Grandma took in washing from white people who would bring their laundry to her one day and pick it up two days later.

2.22 MY 5TH BIRTHDAY:

My Mama Olivia's oldest brother, my **Uncle Jessie Williams,** gave me a Joe Louis and Max Schmelling plastic doll pull-toy as a birthday present on my 5th birthday. When I pulled the toy, the plastic dolls, which faced each other, would bump heads and swing their arms as if they were boxing. Somebody told me that Joe Louis was the better and stronger of the two. At that time, I did recognize the difference in their coloring and features but it didn't mean anything to me. I also remember that my **Uncle Jessie** said a lot of good things about the Joe Louis plastic doll, but I don't remember what he said about the Max Schmelling plastic doll.

2.30 ELEMENTARY SCHOOL YEARS:

In 1939, I began elementary school. According to the research of **Dr. Melvin O Smith**, who later became a personal friend, before 1932 the elementary school that I attended had been called the **Campostella School for Coloreds,** and in 1932 it was re-named **The Richard Allen Tucker Elementary School** in honor of a Professor Tucker who was the first black principal of an elementary school in Norfolk.

This school was a red brick structure containing an office, four classrooms, outdoor toilets with running water, and a large playground. Each classroom had a 'pot-belly' coal stove, a teacher's desk, student desks anchored to the wooden floor, book cases or cabinets for teacher supplies, and blackboards around the room. There were large windows and lots of sunlight coming into the classrooms.

I liked all my elementary school teachers, and they acted as if they liked me. My first grade school teacher was Miss Stevenson. I remember the day she explained that an "ass" was a donkey. She did this in a response to a teary-eyed girl's complaint that James Burnham had just told her "to kiss his ass." I thought Miss Stevenson was smart to explain things that way, but by first grade we all knew what James meant. We were all only about six years old, but we all had heard adult curse words. I don't know what happened to James after we both left elementary school.

I remember that I enjoyed reading stories and sounding out words. I think I learned to read quickly. Miss Stephenson seemed to enjoy all of us who read well, and reading just seemed to be fun.

2.40 THE NEW RICHARD A. TUCKER SCHOOL:

In 1942 a new R.A. Tucker School was built in Campostella and so were two major Negro housing areas; Oak-leaf Park and Anderson Park.

The new school had been built about a mile from the old school and it was a "top of the line" structure. The school was a beautiful white cinder-block, one level building with large windows. It had fifteen classrooms, a principal's office, special space for secretaries, a cafeteria, auditorium/gymnasium, art room, vocational work areas, central heat, library, health clinic, book storage rooms, a large playground and indoor toilets. It had been built to accommodate the children of black families who were moving to the Norfolk Metropolitan area to support the war effort. For the first time, I met kids who didn't grow up in Campostella.

2.50 LEARNING "PROPER SPEECH":

When I was 10 years old, my Mama Olivia sent me to the drug store at the corner of Indian River Road and Wilson Road to buy "castor oil." The drug store was owned and operated by white people who seemed friendly and pleasant. On this visit I learned an important lesson. I asked the woman behind the counter for a "bottle of castoil." She looked at me, smiled and asked me, "Sonny, what did you say you wanted?" I said, "A bottle of castoil." This friendly lady smiled and called over her sales-partner and asked me to say again what I wanted. I repeated myself and both of them chuckled softly. The first woman asked, "Sonny, do you mean a bottle of castor oil?" I said, "Yes ma'am, I want a bottle of castor oil."

From that day forward, I try never to speak without thinking about how the words sounded as they came out of my mouth. I learned over time to be as precise as I could when I spoke. Thus far, this tendency has not hurt me.

2.60 GOING CRABBING WITH GRANDMA BELL:

Ever so often, from about March thru October, Grandma Bell would go to the river shore (southern side of the eastern branch of the Elizabeth River in Norfolk) and collect drift wood for firewood. After we collected the drift wood and loaded the pull-carts, Grandma would let us crab. This was fun and most of the time I caught a few small crabs. When we returned home, we would cook the crabs and have a feast; at least it seemed like a feast to me. It dawned on me early on that Grandma and Granddaddy Bell were poor and needed this driftwood for fuel to keep them warm. When the wood supply in their back yard got low, Grandma would again take us (her grandchildren) to help collect and bring back driftwood.

Grandpa Bell was blind, but he would cut (with a saw) the driftwood and neatly stack it up to have it ready for burning. Sometimes he would go to the river-shore with us just to help with the heavily loaded pull-cart.

2.70 Visiting Grandmama Williams on Sundays

Many Sundays my mother would let Madeline (my oldest sister) and me go to visit her mother (Grandma Williams) and we would play with our aunts who were our same ages. Madeline and I had to cross the main street of Campostella called Wilson Road to get to Grandmama Williams' house. Wilson Road was a busy traffic-bearing street that separated "main Campostella" from the "over-the-field" section of Campostella. The walk from our house to Grandma Williams' house was about one and a half miles.

Granddaddy Daniel (DEE) Williams was not around much on Sundays. I understood that he was the pastor of a church in the "New Light" part of Virginia Beach or whatever. When I did see him, most of the time he would be sitting at the kitchen table eating alone. I never saw him eat with anyone. Grandma Williams would sit at the table with him, but I never saw her eat while he was eating. After Granddaddy Williams ate, my aunts and uncles would go into the kitchen and get their food and bring it back to the table in the family room and eat.

I don't remember having a "thinking" conversation with my Granddaddy Williams as I had with my Granddaddy (Henry) Bell, but Granddaddy Williams was always smiling and nodding his approval in my direction. The one thing I do remember him telling me after I was designated class valedictorian was, "Junie, I'm proud of you. You're going to do good. Keep it up."

When Mat (Madeline) and I were ready to return home from our Sunday visits to Grandma (Carrie) Williams, she always gave us a nickel for an ice cream cone. We would buy an ice cream cone on Wilson Road, which we had to cross on our way back home, and we would slowly lick our ice cream cones, trying to make them last as long as we could.

2.80 Earning my "first" dollar:

I was about 10 years old when Brother Murphy, an old-time, front-porch, preacher-man who lived down the street from us called to me as I was passing him in his field one morning. He asked me if I wanted to earn some money by helping him plant a field of sweet-potato sprouts. I said yes, and we started planting about 9 0'clock in the morning. When I went home at lunch time for about 30 minutes, I told my mother that I had a day's work to do with Brother Murphy and she seemed pleased. I went back after lunch and Brother Murphy and I continued planting until 6:30 that evening. When we finished, he looked at me thoughtfully and then looked out at the large field where the sprouts were planted. He put his hand in his pocket, pulled out a one dollar bill and gave it to me. He told me "good work." I was as happy as I could be. I ran all the way home to let my Mama see the dollar bill.

2.90 When Mama Olivia died:

I was 11 years old when my Mama, Olivia Williams Bell, died, and that was the end of my carefree childhood. Mama had been on her way to Christmas shopping and a car hit her as she crossed Wilson Road to catch a bus. It was a simple, tragic accident. We buried Mama on Christmas Eve, 1944, and on that same Christmas Eve night, Madeline, my older sister, and I helped Daddy to play Santa Claus to our four younger sisters.

Before Mama Olivia's death, I had taken her for granted. She was a steady and sure presence in my growing up just like the sunrise in the morning or the streetlights that came on every night. But Mama's death made me aware, in a child's way, that there was a curtain between me and another world that surrounded me and that that world was stocked with things I had never thought about. I didn't cry at Mama's funeral because I knew (in my child's mind) that I would get to see her again; either in heaven or back here again in this world. My thoughts were: all I had to do was to be a good boy, do my best to help my Daddy care for my younger sisters, and I'd get to see my Mama again.

My mother's death placed a serious burden on everybody, especially my Dad and my older sister. I speak of these factors in other parts of this book. There were lots of things that I don't remember about my Mama, but some of the things I do remember about her are noted in Appendix A.

3.0 EARLY ADOLESCENT REMEMBRANCES

3.10 RACIAL AWARENESS:

At about 12 years old, I became aware of the privileges assigned to white people and the reality of segregation. I became aware without fanfare or shock. Racial segregation was simply a way of life that was accepted by all as how the world and the people in it were created and assigned to be. Many black people may have thought segregation was wrong, but from age 12 thru age 18, I didn't hear a voice raised about doing anything to change it. From about the age of 13, my awareness of white privilege prompted me to be suspicious of the motives of most of the white people I met. I was also watchful, if not suspicious, of light-complexioned black people, because I sensed that they thought that they were better than darker-skinned blacks.

3.20 CONVERSATIONS WITH GRANDPA (HENRY) BELL:

Grandpa Bell was blind. He didn't go to church and when I was about 12 years old we began discussing the Bible. Grandpa Bell knew I was getting serious about studying religion and he would ask me questions in a way that I hadn't considered. Grandpa Bell would ask questions such as, "Did Adam (the first man) have a navel?" "Was Jonah swallowed by a big fish or a whale?" "Could a man live in the stomach of such a creature for 3 days?" "Could it have rained all over the earth as told in the Noah story?" "Could a woman have a baby without the help of a sperm from a man?"

As I think back, I can see that Grandpa (Henry) Bell was not a Christian, in the common use of the word Christian. This is because he posed the most un-Christian-like questions. But Grandpa Bell made me think about the things that were written in the Bible. At 13, I knew that most of the stories in the Bible were myths, grown-up fairy tales, but I still thought that they taught worthwhile messages except when the Jews' Jehovah God told the Hebrews to kill other people and to take their land and to mistreat them. And from observation, I knew that at 13 years of age, I needed to be quiet about my real feelings on these matters or the old people of the church would not like you.

3.30 MY SISTERS:

3.31 MARJORIE MADELINE:

Before Mama died, I had thought of Madeline, my older sister, not as a girl but as just another playmate. After Mama died, I saw Madeline as a big sister and as a young teenager who was now doing a woman's job in trying to take care of the house. Madeline became the chief care-taker for our younger sisters. My job was to wash dishes, clean the house, scrub the floors, cut wood, bring in coal for the fire, and work with Madeline to keep the house working when Dad wasn't at home. I did what I could to help Mat (Marjorie's nick-name) with the responsibilities that Dad had placed on her and to help her adjust to the restrictions he had made on her teen-age, social life. Mat and I became friends and not just a brother and a sister unit who happened to live in the same house.

3.32 MY YOUNGER SISTERS:

All my younger sisters were little ladies. There was **Olivia, Lillie, Martha, and Jessie** and each of them had different personalities. From what I can remember, they treated me well and I did my best to return their consideration. I baby-sat them from the time I was 11 until I was 14 years old. When I was 14, my Dad married Mama Elsie and I didn't have to baby-sit anymore. I think I thought of my sisters as being baby girls during my stay at home. I do remember that Olivia would volunteer to be my accident-patient when I needed to practice my Boy Scout first aid skills.

3.33 WORKING IN THE FIELDS:

We planted and harvested sweet potatoes, green beans, butter beans, and cabbages in several fields surrounding or near our house. My younger sisters worked in the fields picking butter beans or green beans. I helped Dad to plant and harvest sweet potatoes. I cleaned the chicken house, or weeded the grass (with a hoe) from between-the rows in the fields. I didn't have much of a problem doing farm-work, but my little sisters did not like this type of work and sometimes they cried when they had to go into the fields and pick butter beans or string beans.

3.40 MEETING GIRLS FOR THE FIRST TIME:

By the time I was thirteen or fourteen, I felt that all the neighborhood girls liked me. I felt this way because they would treat me very friendly-like. This made me feel good. However, I noticed that at school (elementary), the girls were smarter than the boys in reading, in math, and in most other studies. I also remember how the girls teased the boys and made us run after them. I enjoyed their teasing but I did not do any running after them. Many of the other boys enjoyed running after them and I noticed that many times the girls slowed down so that the boys could catch them.

4.0 COUSINS, AUNTS, AND UNCLES

I grew up with many cousins and aunts and a few uncles. They all treated me well or helped me to feel "good and comfortable" about myself.

4.10 COUSINS:

I got to know and play with my cousins who were the children of my Dad's sister, **Aunt Geneva "Pigeon" Hawkins**. I played with **Neal, Robert, Freddie, and Bradford.** Their sisters, **Claudette and Annette** were too young to play with me, and so I really didn't get to know them.

In addition to my Hawkins cousins, I had cousins **Myrtle Bell (daughter of Aunt Lillie (Aunt Bayby)) and William Bell (son of Aunt Willie (Aunt Mutt))**. As a pre-teenager, I spent lots of time playing with all my cousins as well as with the other neighborhood children. I don't remember a significant disagreement or fight between me and them during our playtime together. We all (cousins and childhood friends) played "Cowboys and Indians" or "U.S. Commandos against Japanese soldiers" or we made-believe we were super-heroes fighting outer-space, earth-invaders or some dragon or monster. We played with toy cars and pull wagons. We shot marbles "for keeps"; a game where each player would put an equal number of marbles in a ring drawn on the ground and then compete to knock marbles out of the ring with a "shooter" marble. It was a game of skill, because each "shooter" would keep all the marbles he knocked out of the ring. We played stickball in the street and sometimes we played "smoot," a card game. The girls played with the boys up until they were 11 or 12 years old. I've always had and kept good feelings about all my cousins, and I believed they had good feelings for me.

4.20 AUNTS:

My dad had four sisters. There was **Aunt Baybye,** whom I didn't get to know because she died when I was very young. My Dad's other sisters were **Aunt Willie Bell, Aunt Geneva (Pigeon) Hawking, and Auntie (Martha) Kellam.** I got to know only one of them; **Auntie (Martha) Kellam**. My **Aunt Kellam** was a hard-working church lady and she was always warm and welcoming to me.

My mother (Olivia Williams) had nine sisters and five brothers. Her sisters were **Virginia, Daisy, Helen, Carrie, Janie, Doris, Rebecca, Thelma and Sarah.** Most of these aunts were too old to be my playmate except for **Doris, Rebecca, Thelma and Sarah.** When I visited Grandma Williams on Sundays, I played mostly with **Doris, Rebecca (Beck)** and **Thelma (Scoopy). Sarah** was too young to be my playmate.

4.30 UNCLES:

My dad had an older brother whom I called **Uncle Bell**. I remember the times Dad would borrow Uncle Bell's horse (Maggie) to plow our fields. **Uncle Bell** didn't talk much to children, including me, and he didn't go to church either, like my Dad (his brother). **Uncle Bell** lived on Pike Street (directly across from our house) and on Sunday afternoons he would be sitting in the rocking chair on his front porch when my sisters and I came back from church. I always wondered why he and my Dad seemed so different about going to church.

My mother Olivia, in addition to her sisters, had five (5) brothers; **Uncles: Jesse, Benjamin (Ben), Daniel, Michael (Mike), and Welton.** All of them, except for **Welton**, had been drafted into the army during World War II. **Ben and Daniel** told me about how they served as longshoremen during the Allied invasion of Sicily and how they had to take ammunition from their ship to the beach in small boats and collect the bodies of dead American soldiers and move them into temporary holding areas on the invasion beach. **Jesse and Mike** didn't talk about their army experiences.

I got to know **Uncle Jesse and Uncle Welton** better than the others. When I was in college, I had serious conversations with each of them about race and religion. They both seemed wise and thoughtful and were very critical of black people, white people, and of the U.S. government in particular. In our discussions, they both made it clear to me that they thought that religion was holy-foolishness and that black preachers were taking advantage of poor, superstitious black people. They felt that way in spite of the fact that their Daddy, my granddaddy, was the pastor of a Baptist church. I liked our discussions and most of the time I agreed with them but sometimes I would argue against them, just to hear them make their points.

5.0 BOY SCOUTING

I became a boy scout when I was 12 years old. I was serious about becoming an eagle scout and being good so that God would give me back my mother (who had been killed in an automobile accident). I loved boy-scouting. There was so much to learn from the scout merit-badges books and I liked the scout uniform. From my scouting, I remember the people I admired and who kept me energized to be a good scout. They were:

My first Scoutmaster, **Edgar J. Ellis; m**y second Scoutmaster, **Paul Northern;, m**y first Asst. Scoutmaster, **Curtis Fulford;** and my first patrol leader (Swallow Patrol), **Eugene Joyner** were all good and warm-hearted people. The other members of my Scout patrol were **Melvin Smith** (who later became an Ed.D.), **William Bell** (my cousin), **Norsmen Hinds** (my first philosophical discussion friend), **Allen Clarke, and George Ricks**.

There was a group of senior (older boys) scouts that I admired and respected from their bearing and politeness. That group consisted of **Rudolph Boone** (Troop bugler), **Lloyd Ricks, James (Juice) Johnson, Willie Clarke,** the **Simpson** brothers **(Andrea and Melvin), and the brothers, Floyd and Willie Williams of Boy Scout #80.**

At sixteen, I attained the rank of Life-Scout and earned 27 scout merit badges. I didn't become an Eagle scout because I did not acquire the "Cooking" merit badge. I worked with two other scouts in trying to meet the cooking merit badge requirements but we never could please the cooking merit badge counselor enough for him to award us the merit badge. The cooking merit badge counselor was the Scoutmaster of another Boy Scout Troop, and he made things difficult for boys from other troops to move ahead of his own scouts.

This was an early lesson in learning to deal with losing when you think you should be winning. When I became a high-school senior (at 16 years old), I suddenly loss interest in scouting and didn't bother any more with trying to get the cooking merit badge.

6.0 Mama Elsie comes into our lives

About three years after my mother Olivia died, my dad married Elsie Armstrong, a girl he'd known in his youth. My sisters and I called her "Mama Elsie," and for me, calling her "Mama Elsie" came easy. I liked Mama Elsie from the start. Her coming to live with us was a joy. I say much more about Mama Elsie in Appendix C.

7.0 Jr. High and High School Recollections of note

7.10 THE BIG, BIG SCHOOL:

In 1946, at 13 years of age, I entered Booker T. Washington (BTW) Junior High School in Norfolk, Virginia. The Junior high school was in a separate section of the large factory-like building that also housed the high school. Booker T. Washington (BTW) junior/high school was a large white brick school with three floors, a large auditorium, and a large gymnasium. BTW was the only public Negro high school in Norfolk, Virginia.

I had to catch a city bus to get from Campostella to BTW which was located in the all-black area of the Brambleton section of Norfolk. To me, a boy from "over the field," Norfolk and BTW were big places. For me, junior high school was a new world and turned out to be fun.

7.20 ENTERING HIGH SCHOOL:

I was 14 years old when I entered BTW high school in 1947. According to the dominant school rumors at that time, BTW had the best marching band and the best choir, bar none, in the state of Virginia. I was really in a big fish bowl where everybody seemed older, bigger, and more mature than I. This meant that I had to be cautious and watch the student leaders around me as a guide to staying out of trouble or not making enemies. I did a good job of doing just that and I negotiated my way pass lots of potential problems with other students. The big people on the school campus were the athletes, the band members, the choir members, and the student fraternity/sorority members. I was never big on the high school campus.

7.30 SANDLOT SPORTS:

I played sandlot football and softball, and also played basketball as a team-member of the "Campostella Panthers" in the Norfolk Community Recreation League. We, the Campostella Panthers, never won a championship in anything while I was a team member, but we won enough to always be in contention or in a runner-up position. I was always on the starting squad of all the teams. I was a guard in basketball, a line-backer (on defense) and a left halfback (on offense) in football. We used the single-wing running formation, because we had not been introduced to the newly developing "T" formation. Our team colors were red and black.

Some of the outstanding Campostella Panthers softball team members included **Otis Butts, Garland Johnson, Allen Clark**, (all pitchers); **Araf Cuffee**, (first base); **William Bell,** (catcher and my cousin); **Pernell Moore, Leroy "Buck" Jones, Junius Floyd, Melvin "Peter Joe" Smith** (all outfielders); **George Ricks** (shortstop); **Chris Bell** (the author) third base; **Theodore Clarke** (second base); and **Cutty Cuffee**, who was an all-around substitute.

Some of the outstanding Campostella Panthers football team members were:

William Bell (my cousin), **Melvin Smith, Roy Massey,** as tackles; **Araf Cuffee,** quarterback; **Junius Floyd**, extremely talented, as right half back; and **Billy Parsons**, a terrific pass-receiving left end. I was a sure-fire tackler and a good runner (half-back) on offense.

7.40 MR. PAUL ROBESON'S APPEARANCE DURING MY HIGH SCHOOL SENIOR YEAR:

Mr. Paul Robeson, the world famous singer and **actor,** came to BTW high school and favored us students with his singing. He favored us because he had been in the Norfolk area and had been a college buddy of our principal, **Mr. Winston Douglas.** I was fascinated by Robeson's acappella singing of **Old Man River, Water Boy, and Danny Boy.** My Dad loved those three songs and sings them around the house all the time. When I told him about Mr. Robeson coming to our high school, I remember him smiling and asking me if Mr. Robeson sounded like him when he sang. I said yes and we both laughed.

7.50 VIRGINIA STATE BOYS STATE, 1949:

In 1949, along with several other boys from Booker T. Washington High school and Saint Joseph High school, I was invited to attend the first Virginia State Boys State Camp for Colored boys. This was when I first sensed that somebody had been watching me without me being aware of their watching. I was already thinking that I was smart as far as academics and scouting were concerned, but now I sensed somebody else also had that suspicion. The Virginia State Boys State Camp took place at Virginia State College in Petersburg, Virginia and lasted a week. It was an education and sports camp. On the next to the last day, the majority of the participants voted for me to be a Supreme Court Justice of the fictitious "boys state."

7.60 CLASS VALEDICTORIAN, FEB 1950:

Early in Jan of 1950, my homeroom teacher, **Miss Fannie M. Jones** told me that I was the "class valedictorian." I asked her what was a valedictorian? She smiled and said that I had the highest grade-point average among all the seniors who were graduating with me. I was delighted with the news, but figured I should act like it wasn't anything big. However**, the Norfolk Journal and Guide** (newspaper) made my becoming valedictorian its front page news story with pictures of me and the 10 girls who were also honor students. At this point, my family, friends, and others started acting like I had done something special, especially for a person who lived "over the field" in Campostella; of all places.

8.0 THE RAMBLINGS OF MY TEENAGE MIND

8.1 WATCHING OLDER TEEN-AGERS AND ADULTS:

I became interested in the female body quite early; about 13-14 years of age. I began noticing that girls were attractive and most of the time they smelled good and powdery, and they gave me bright smiles. Their happy dispositions allowed my imagination about them to soar and expand to see myself as a knight coming to their rescue or as their hero and meeting them in romantic, faraway places; just like in the movies.

8.20 MY PRETTY TEACHERS AND SKIN COLOR:

Many of my junior high and high school teachers were pretty and they had all types of colorings; dark chocolate, light chocolate, caramel, lemon, and vanilla. It was during my teacher-admiration period (Ages 13-16) of development that I began noticing skin color and the importance this factor had on many of my classmates; and maybe on me. Also at this time, I began registering that many light-complexioned girls and darker complexion girls separated themselves into their respective groups. Somehow I knew color had something to do with their separating into groups, but the boys were different. We boys played and interacted and color didn't enter the picture. I wasn't bothered about this new awakening on my part. I instinctively knew that color didn't really matter when judging people.

9.0 FRESHMAN AND SOPHOMORE COLLEGE YEARS

9.10 COLLEGE BOY:

I was the first person in the Bell family to go to college. When I first went to Norfolk Division of Virginia State College (called Little State), I was seventeen. I had no problems fitting into the student population even though male students generally wore shirts and ties that gave the college a serious business-like, adult appearance. I became a member of the student debate team and student government. I did pretty well in my studies too.

9.20 RELIGIOUS EMPHASIS WEEK:

At Little State, chapel attendance once a week on Mondays was mandatory. During one week (5 consecutive days at noon) of the spring semester, Little State hosted a noted clergyman as a guest speaker. We called that week our "Religious Emphasis Week." The two speakers who visited Little State and sermonized during the two years I was there were **Reverend Vernon Johns** (spring'50) and **Reverend Dr. Samuel Proctor** (spring'51). After listening to each of them, I knew that I wanted to learn to speak and to hold an audience's attention in the same way that they held my attention. These two preachers did not resort to myths in their sermonizing, but each made me think seriously about what my priorities should be as a black college male student living in a white controlled country. Both of them made it clear that education was the only power the black man could get and use to free himself from white domination.

9.30 WRITING FOR THE COLLEGE-PAPER:

At Little State, I partnered with **Wilbur Chadwick**, a fellow young philosopher, and we began a cartoon and commentary article series for the student newspaper. I would write the article and **Wilbur** would draw an accompanying cartoon. We did two such articles for the student newspaper. **Wilbur** and I became life-long friends.

9.40 STUDENT OF THE ISSUE:

Because of my participation in student activities, I was selected "Student of the Quarter" during one semester and received a front page write-up in the student newspaper. I felt good about that.

9.50 SUMMER WORK AT THE PICKLE FACTORY:

Fortunately, there was a "Best Foods" pickle factory on the outskirts of Campostella. During two consecutive summers, I managed to get work there. This was a blessing because the pickle factory also provided work for many other black students and adults who might otherwise would have remained unemployed.

10.0 Junior and Senior college years

In February 1952, I transferred from "Little State" to "Big State" (Virginia State College in Petersburg, Virginia). I was now a little fish in a big, big fish bowl.

10.10 THE ROTC SUMMER CAMP:

The ROTC Summer Camp of 1952 for Va. State ROTC Cadets was held at Fort Lee, Virginia. The summer camp training was 6 weeks of sweaty work with basic military training, but it was also lots of fun. This camp was the first time that I and my cadet-classmates had the opportunity to live with and see up-close white guys our age. Virginia State ROTC cadets were billeted with the all-white, ROTC cadets from the University of Pittsburg. We were housed in World War II army barracks. I must say that Virginia State cadets were very competitive in every military skill and practice. I felt good about that, and I learned "close up" that Virginia State cadets were as good as or better than all of the white ROTC cadets in the whole summer camp!

When school opened the following September (1952), along with several other cadets, I was awarded the Distinguished Military Student (DMS) Badge. I was also promoted to Cadet major and assigned as the regimental adjutant; a position that was unique during regimental parades. ROTC was fun and easy, and military classes were generally commonsense exercises after the basic military teaching points had been explained. Eventually I was promoted to Cadet Lt. Colonel. Yes, ROTC was fun.

10.20 SO THIS IS A FRATERNITY?

In the spring of 1953, I was accepted as a pledgee in the "NU PSI" chapter (Va. State) of the Omega Psi Phi Fraternity. I went "Omega" because the high goals of the fraternity attracted me and I admired a few of the fellows in that fraternity. Along with the other "dogs" (pledgees) on my line, I "caught hell." Our "dog-master" was a brutish fellow who made it a point to strike a pledgee upon the least provocation. In 1953, joining Omega at Virginia State involved letting your "big brothers" beat you with a strap or paddle as hard as they could or until another "big brother" told them to stop or until one of your dog-brothers volunteered to take the remainder of your pending licks. I took these beatings along with the other dogs, but vowed I would never behave as my big brothers were behaving by inflicting pain on another person.

I became disillusioned with my Omega big brothers when they beat one of my dog-brothers so badly with a leather strap and a wooden paddle that his buttocks swelled, burst, and bled; and many of them laughed about it when he had to go to the college hospital. This injured and beaten dog-brother was very light-skinned and could have easily passed for a white man. When he was on his way to the hospital, I overheard one of the "big brothers" commenting without sympathy about his white-ass complexion. My injured dog-brother could not continue the initiation process and did not "get over" and become an Omega-man. I think this was when I decided that this fraternity's behavior was not really like its high ideals, and not what I had hoped it would be. As soon as I "made it over" and got my picture taken and my certificate as proof of membership, I stopped formal activity with the fraternity and I've been inactive ever since.

10.30 ACADEMIC PROBATION:

Except for ROTC, I did poorly as a student during the fall semester of 1952 and the spring semester of 1953. I was not able to do well because I had personal problems that troubled my mind and could not study with the enthusiasm required to be a good chemistry student. In short, I did not maintain a C average in chemistry (my major) and I failed in calculus. I was placed on "Academic Probation" at the end of my junior year, and my academic record bears this notation.

10.40 MARRYING BLANCHE ONEAL JONES:

In May of 1953, at twenty (20) years old, I married **Blanche Oneal Jones**, a girl whom I had been dating since I was 16 years old. Blanche and I stayed married for over 22 years, but we separated in 1972 and divorced in 1975. Our marriage resulted in the birth and ensuing joy of four beautiful children: **Chris III, Kevin, Kathleen, and Keith.**

10.50 MISSING MY COLLEGE GRADUATION CEREMONY:

After my marriage to Blanche, I went back to college (September 1953) and concentrated on my studies. I was behind and had to "catch-up" and "keep up" at the same time in order to graduate on time. I had to repeat a chemistry course, including the laboratory work, and repeat a calculus course. For me, college was work, work, and more work!

I wasn't able to graduate on time with my fellow classmates. I could not catch up and finish my chemistry laboratory experiments in time. Unfortunately, I had to watch from a 3rd floor window of Colson Hall (Science building) as my classmates and their families celebrated their graduation and paraded on the campus green; a sad day in my memory.

I spent the next week and a half, night and day, in the Colson Hall chemistry laboratory completing laboratory experiments and recording and reporting my data to the professor. I took my last report, my analysis of an unknown alloy to the professors' home for his approval of my findings. He took my report back into his home office and came back and told me I had done a "pretty good job" in detecting the identities and the amounts of the several elements that were combined in the alloy. He said he would notify the college registrar that I had successfully fulfilled all my chemistry requirements. He then congratulated me on dutifully earning a bachelor degree in chemistry. He shook my hand and wished me good luck.

10.60 WORKING AT THE SHIPYARD:

After belatedly completing my college graduation requirements, I worked at Colonna Shipyard which was located on the Berkley side of the railroad tracks on the outskirts of Campostella. The work was physically hard, heavy, dirty, and mud-sloshing. Sometimes we hand-painted and cleaned the insides of naval ships and on one occasion we worked at cleaning the inside compartments of a petroleum tanker. I worked side-by-side with the regular crew; a group of older black men. We wore knee-boots and worked with shovels, scrapers, ropes and pulleys and much of the work required hands-on lifting, pulling, and pushing.

I could see in the eyes of my fellow-workers that they knew they would be working here in this mud and grime for life. But I could also see that they were all thankful to have a job. I was now 21 years old and now I knew that to have work, even hard work, and to make enough to feed your family was a blessing. I worked beside these hard working, poor, and mostly proud men for the two and one-half months it took for my commissioning to become official and my first military orders to arrive. I'll never forget these men and what I gathered about them from our daily conversations. Although life was hard for them, I sensed that they continued to hope and pray that better days would be coming; if they trusted in the Lord.

11.0 MY MILITARY CAREER; THE FIRST 10 YEARS

I received my college diploma by mail in August 1954 and was commissioned a second lieutenant in the US Army in September 1954. I went on active duty 22 November 1954 at Fort Lee, Virginia; and boy was I happy! I considered myself lucky to have graduated, and more than ever, I knew after four years of college that I was not smart; no, I was just lucky.

11.10 MILITARY TRAVELS AND DUTY ASSIGNMENTS:

Making "soldiering" my career was an easy decision. I really didn't know what I wanted to be or do when I graduated from college. In college, I had come to dislike chemistry and science in general. When I got in the military, I liked the experiences of military travel and of meeting different people in different cultures. I also enjoyed carrying out my military duties and responsibilities because I always had the feeling that I was doing something important.

Early in my military career, I was convinced that I was good at my job and that there was no lieutenant or captain in the US Army who was a better soldier. In my first assignment overseas, in Pusan, Korea (1955-1957), I was especially inspired to remain in the army because of the following three Negro officers:

Captain Clyde J. Davis (QMC) who was my company commander. Captain Davis was tall, big, and tough-looking. He had a bravado that required you to listen clearly when he "suggested" that you do something. Davis had a joking and fatherly spirit when at leisure, but he had a no nonsense demeanor when it came to getting the job done. He shared stories about himself when he was a lieutenant in Germany after WWII.

Captain Edward H. Soule (INF): who was the Battalion Operations officer. He had been a member of the all black, 555th Paratrooper Brigade. Captain Soule's jokes, and his spit and polished appearance impressed me. He shared stories of his experiences in the army when it was segregated in the early 1950s;

Major Richard W. Spikes, (QMC) who was my battalion (142 QM Battalion) commander. I was impressed by his "watch me" poise and demeanor; his probing questions during Officer Calls; and his pronunciation of his words as he gave instructions.

CHRISTOPHER C. BELL JR., ED.D.

Separately these officers would say, "We need lieutenants like you to stay in the military and be good officers." They felt that it was the black soldier and his ability to be as good at soldiering that first impressed and started white men thinking of black people as people who are due more respect; maybe even in America.

11.11 BACK WHEN WE CALLED IT RACISM:

I didn't really have to be convinced much to remain in the army. The headlines of several editions of the Stars and Stripes newspaper (1956-57) made me aware of the "Massive Resistance to school desegregation" that was going on in Virginia. I certainly didn't want to go back to Virginia, my home state, and work as a teacher; so the army fitted me fine.

I did not come face to face with hostile, violent racism, but in my travels across the country, I had to use the "Green Book" as a travel guide. The Green Book was a tourist guide book for Colored travelers. The book listed locations of overnight accommodations (usually hosted by black people) that would accept Colored travelers. The Green book stayed in fashion until the early 1960s.

With regards to racism in the military itself in 1954, the army was mostly racially integrated at the company levels if not at the staff levels. In all my duty assignments, except for one small, isolated occasion, I had no race-related personnel problems in supervising white and black soldiers. Was I luckier than most black lieutenants? Perhaps, I don't know. The mind-set of the American white man and white soldier was rapidly changing from being the "anointed determiner" of the world order to being in partnership with other countries in determining "world order." The use of diplomacy in dealing with third world nations was beginning to bud. Hah, the world order was changing. We know this now by hind-sight. This changing in the world order began when America did not win the Korean War. The Korean War was the first American military expedition in which America fought a "developing" nation and did not win.

I encountered racism in finding suitable "off base housing" near Fort MacArthur, California, (1955), and at Fort Lee, Virginia (1958). During these time-frames most white property or apartment owners did not rent apartments to black people if their apartment/properties already contained white tenants. This white-owner racial bias began vanishing at the start of the Vietnam War (1963).

11.12 OVERSEAS TRAVELS:

My wife Blanche and our children (Chris III, Kevin, and Kathleen) accompanied me overseas to several duty stations; twice to Europe (Germany and France), and to Africa (Ethiopia). I believe our foreign travels and living environments were very beneficial to my children in rounding out their ability to meet and relate to people, and allowing them to feel good about themselves as first-class people.

I've written down some of my thoughts and feelings about military life in a book of poems entitled **"Soldiers Do Reason Why. . ."** This book is described in Appendix F of this autobiography. I recommend the book to the reader who wishes to know more about my thoughts and considerations as I was being awakened to the realities of a wide world that existed beyond America's shores and definitions of life.

12.0 My military career; the second 10 years

12.10 MILITARY DUTIES:

My military training and duties made me what the military called a "Logistics Officer." A logistics officer is required to have expertise in overseeing and directing personnel in the management of the flow (movement, proper storage, accounting for, and control) of materials such as general supplies, food and equipment, ammunition, petroleum, etc.) from the time these materials enter the military supply system, until it is delivered to front line army units. I was an expert at my job.

12.20 FAILURE TO BE PROMOTED:

When the time came for me to be promoted from captain to major, I was passed over (not promoted). I went to the Pentagon to inquire about my status and was told that my efficiency report just before being considered for promotion had placed me in the "excellent range" (93-96 out of 100) while my contemporaries who were promoted had efficiency reports that placed them in the "superior range" (97-100 out of 100).

Through military review channels I administratively challenged the less than superior rating that kept me from being promoted with my contemporaries, but I was unsuccessful. As quiet as it may be kept, at that time (up until the beginning of the Vietnam War era (1965) the "honest assessment" of black army officers by many white army officers was that black officers, even those who do well, were not in the 97-100 zone of efficiency and they reserved such a rating zone for other white officers. It just so had happened that I had the career misfortune of working for such an "honest assessment" type of white commanding officer. Also unfortunately for me, the key officer who could have substantiated my allegation of being unfairly rated was another black officer who worked for the same commanding officer against whom I complained. This black officer's testimony was a punctilious, non-informational, "I saw little, I heard little, and I know nothing," and as a result I wasn't able to prove to the satisfaction of the Military Review Board that adjudicated my complaint that I had been unfairly rated. Needless to say, my complaint did not endear me to the local military gentry.

12.40 A NEW UNDERSTANDING OF GETTING PROMOTED:

I knew now that knowing and doing your job in an outstanding manner is not the key to success in any organization. The key to success is to be average in job efficiency but to be very efficient in grooming one's relationship with one's supervisors. Once I understood this truth, I stopped being creative and became a "group-think, supervisor-grooming" officer.

Once I applied this knowledge, my career moved forward. During the last 8 years of my career, all of my ratings were in the "superior" range and I was awarded the following performance-of-duty medals: **The Army Commendation Medal** for service at Ft. Devens (1966-1967)**; The Bronze Star Medal** for service in Vietnam (1967-1968); **The Army Meritorious Service Medal** for service at Ft. Devens (1968-1970); **The Army Meritorious Service Medal with Oak leaf cluster** for service in Ethiopia (1970-1972)**; and the Army Commendation Medal with Oak leaf cluster** for service in Korea (1973-1974).

12.50 READJUSTMENT OF GOALS:

In light of my failure to be promoted with my contemporaries, I knew that whatever genius I may possess, it would not be allowed to show itself while I was in the army. This meant that while in the army I had to start preparing for civilian life. With that in mind, while still in the army I went to school at night and took leave-time when necessary to acquire a Master of Education Degree (M.Ed.) from Fitchburg State University 1969-1970) which was located near my post at Fort Devens, Mass.

13.0 FORWARD MARCH TO CIVILIAN LIFE

13.10 ARMY RETIREMENT AND BACK TO SCHOOL:

I retired from the army, 30 November 1974. Out of 20 years of military service, I served overseas for 14 years and 7 months. When I retired from the army my sense of my future was that of a man being allowed into a new world after passing through a trial period. I felt the military had prepared me for whatever my life's real purpose might turn out to be. I could not define what that purpose might be, but I knew it was in line with making black and white people less fearful of each other and to help educate them in ways that would promote racial justice and cooperation. I felt extremely lucky and I had the strange feeling of being on the way to becoming fully empowered toward making a difference in race relationships. But where this feeling would take me, I did not know, but I had no fear.

Two months before retiring from the army, I took leave and entered (September 1974) Harvard University Graduate School of Education and subsequently earned a Certificate of Advance Study (CAS) in Administration, Planning, and Social Policy in June, 1975.

In April of 1975, I was accepted by Boston University Graduate School of Education as a candidate for a doctoral degree. Fortunately, I had applied for and received (April 1975) a Ford Foundation Fellowship that would pay my tuition, book expenses, and a small monthly stipend. It seemed as though the stars and planets had aligned in some way to bless me! I completed my doctoral requirements, including my dissertation by May 1978. My major was Organizational Development.

I knew I was blessed to have attended the universities noted above and I also knew I had to "give back" some value in service to the forces, people, agencies, and circumstances that allowed me to attend them. My sense of this obligation was not a heavy load. My present life's mission is a part of this obligation and it is described in Bits and Pieces 20.0.

13.20 MY DISSERTATION:

In 1974-1978, while I was in graduate school in Boston, the city of Boston experienced many school-related, racial desegregation problems. These problems presented many points of inquiry for dissertation explorations. My dissertation was entitled: **"Are University-Public School Collaborative Working: an attitudinal survey of Teachers, Selected Parents, and Students of a large Urban High**

School in Boston Mass, May 1978." To minimize the discord and parental demonstrations at several schools that were ordered to integrate, the Federal Judge overseeing Boston's school desegregation case ordered selected University in the Boston metropolitan area to form a partnership with selected high school that were feeling the stress of racially integrating. The thinking was that universities with their professors and educational experts would be able to assist public school personnel in dealing with disgruntled parents and emotionally upset students and help move the process of integrated education in a positive direction.

To obtain data on the success of this project, I observed, designed a survey to account for selected characteristic that would indicate project "pluses or minuses"; surveyed selected teachers, parents, and students of Brighton High School in Boston MA; visited South Boston High School (the central location of white parents' protests); interviewed several black students and social studies teachers; visited the black community of Roxbury to interview black parents whose children were attempting to integrate South Boston High School; and attended two Boston School Board meetings to gain an understanding of the dynamics between the white anti-integrationists and the black pro-integrationists on the board.

My dissertation findings suggested that universities in partnership with public schools; (a) could do very little to influence the quality of education or educational outcomes in public schools, and (b) could do little to diminish white parental discontent and demonstrations against the implementation of forced desegregation of the public schools, and (c) public school teachers/ personnel saw college professors as know-nothings and out of touch intruders.

In traveling about Boston in 1976 and 1977, I saw for the first time the rough conditions under which many black people live in a large American northern city. What I saw, especially in several high-rise apartment buildings in Roxbury, was a way of life that was harsh, dirty, and barely above a subsistence level; all of this poverty and hurt was within a mile radius from the flourishing white dominated downtown section of the city. I was awakened to the black and white patterns of thinking and living that were not evident to me when I was living in the protective cocoon of a military community. The military ideals and way of life served to protect and preserve the dignity and equal privileges of its black members. This is not the case in civilian life. What I witnessed in Boston showed me that black people faced an everyday, harsh, segregated, poverty-bound, struggle to feel like they were human beings. And these remembrances are with me on a daily basis.

14.0 Civilian life and work

14.10 INSIDE THE US DEPARTMENT OF LABOR:

Upon completion of graduate school (May 1978), I began working at the U.S. Department of Labor in Boston, MA, as a Manpower Developer in the Comprehensive Employment and Training Act (CETA) Programs division. The mission of the division was to help low income or unemployed people get training and employment or better jobs. I enjoyed the work and my assignment centered on the workers and the programs in Hartford, Conn, which I visited at least once a month. The Black people in Hartford were in the same position vis-à-vis white people and white establishments as Black people were in regards to white people in Boston, and somehow I knew that this federally sponsored effort in which I was engaged wouldn't change the overall situation in Hartford; but it might give hope to a few black people, including me. After about two years in Boston, I responded to a recruitment notice and was selected and transferred to the Department of Labor in Washington DC to work as a team member to write the new Jobs Training Program Act (JTPA) regulations.

14.20 MARRYING SHARON ANN HARTNETT FORAND:

In 1977, while in graduate school, I became engaged to **Sharon Ann Harnett Forand.** After a three year engagement, Sharon and I married in June 1980 and moved from Boston to Maryland (within the Washington, DC Metropolitan area). We lived together as man and wife for 3 months and then we separated (Sept 1980). Our divorce became final after the legal waiting time period in Maryland.

14.30 UNEMPLOYED AT MIDDLE AGE:

On Dec 30th, 1981, with only 3 years of service in the U.S. Department of Labor, I was involuntarily released (rifted) due to the policies of newly elected President Ronald Reagan who had promised to down-size governmental agencies when he got elected. And so, here I was in Washington D.C. and unemployed at the age 48. But lucky for me, I had a military retirement check every month. However,

THE BITS AND PIECES THAT MAKE ME

even with a military retirement check there is an anxiety that takes hold of an unemployed man who is in need of work, and here I was; unemployed, economically non-productive, disillusioned, and angry.

I can now say that this experience made me acutely aware of how someone feels who is unemployed and who wants to work but cannot find a job. I also learned that in America, a black man's education will not protect him from the wiles of white politics or white economic controls, and that if a black man's employment is not black customer-based, regardless of his education and training, he is vulnerable to white economic controls. Only a few black professionals can rely solely on black people to support them in earning their daily bread; medical doctors, morticians, real estate owners, and clergy members.

14.40 DC PUBLIC SCHOOLS EMPLOYMENT:

I worked as a substitute teacher for the Hyattsville, Maryland school system for about six months until I obtained employment in the District of Columbia Public Schools as an adult education administrator. In this position, I met and worked with many good people. Most of them worked diligently at helping black adults into becoming competent in a variety of trade skills.

14.50 MARRYING SADIE MARIAN HILL WIGGINS:

In the summer of 1982, I met **Sadie Hill Wiggins,** whom I had met over 30 years earlier in Norfolk, Virginia when we were college students. During our meeting this time and over a period of about a year, Sadie and I got to know each other and fell in love. We married December 2, 1983. Today in 2020, after more than 39 years of marriage, we are still together and I still love her.

14.60 CHARLES COUNTY COMMUNITY COLLEGE:

Sensing the opportunity of becoming a college administrator, I resigned from the DC public schools and began working as the Director of the Jobs Training Administration Program (JTPA) at the Charles County Community College in La Plata, Maryland. My responsibilities included coordinating job training and job placement initiatives that served economically disadvantaged persons throughout the three counties of Southern Maryland.

The president of the college and I were the only persons at the college who were working full-time who had doctoral degrees. I had been at the college for a year and a half when the President invited me to a "one on one" afternoon tea. He told me that the college was scheduled for major re-organizing and up-grading. He stated further that I had been at the college for less than two years and that he was committed to promoting the people who had been loyal to him for many years to the new, up-graded positions of responsibility that were scheduled to be created. He said he knew that I would be unhappy with not receiving one of these new positions even though I would probably be highly qualified, and that he did not want me to be on his campus or in his organization and be unhappy. He then suggested (strongly) that I should resign and that he would give me two months advance pay and a letter of recommendation.

After a night's sleep, the next day I resigned. My ambition of a career as a college administrator evaporated.

14.70 FAILURE AT SELLING REAL ESTATE:

I decided now that I'd try a business and get rich. I turned my attention of real estate and became a realtor. In two years I became an assistant broker and was licensed to sell residential property in DC, Maryland, and Virginia. I worked as a realtor for about 4-5 years and failed to make a decent living. I literally went bankrupt. There; I had proved from experience that my way to riches would not and could not be as a real estate sales professional.

14.80 U.S. DEPARTMENT OF EDUCATION:

After a three month job search, I was hired (June 1994) by the U.S. Department of Education as a management analyst. After a year in this position I got promoted to a position that required me to become involved with monitoring the repayment of student loans. This job was boring and unchallenging and I could barely wait to reach my goal of 10 total years of civilian federal service before retiring. I retired in November 2000. I walked into retirement feeling as if I had escaped from prison, but that I had lots of things to do now that would help me to justify the expenses that provided for my doctoral studies. I knew that in some way I would be involved in helping to educate my people (black people) to become psychologically aware of themselves and to start self-improvement projects that would lead to them acquiring authentic self-respect.

15.0 ANOTHER LOOK AT MY SISTERS

My older sister, Marjorie M. Bell Terry died in January 1995 at the age of 63; I was very proud of her. My other sisters are now adults, and I must say that I am proud of them too, all of them. They grew up and showed themselves to be self-reliable, pretty, strong-willed, and smart. All of them have done well or are doing well in the professional paths they chose. They have all treated me well and made me feel that they loved me. I hope that they feel that I did my best to make them feel the same.

16.0 A LOOK AT MY CHILDREN

I have been blessed to have four children and they've all been good to me and good for me. I have briefly described them in the immediate five paragraphs below.

Chris III, my oldest son is an exceptional speaker and writer. He is musically talented, and possesses an engaging personality. Chris is a born leader-type and in many ways he has made me proud of him; especially when he and I have partnered together and performed in musical-sermon programs before UU church audiences. I believe Chris is on his way to making several memorable contributions to the spiritual needs of black people by way of his singing talents, his speaking talents, his volunteer community work, and his teaching skills. I'm proud of him.

Kevin, my second oldest son is steady and sure-footed in all of what he is about. He's also a thinker and I sense sometimes a wonderer. Kevin has always made me proud of his athletic endurance and his self-discipline. In high school, Kevin was a standout in wrestling and track and field. Kevin has always felt he was the best at what he set his mind to do and I agreed with him. He was awarded a full academic scholarship to attend Boston University, and I was proud of him. When Kevin chose the Air Force as a career, I was pleasantly surprised and again I was proud of him. He is a steady dependable trooper.

Kathleen, my beautiful, strong, smart, and personable daughter has always been a joy to me. In school, she was athletic and smart and she earned a four year ROTC College scholarship and she served as an Air Force officer for four years. She has an independent spirit and a go-getter. She is a model of professionalism and warmth to me. At this writing, Kathleen is the principal care-taker of her ailing mother, Blanche Bell; and according to her mother, Kathy is doing an excellent job. I could not have hoped for a more intelligent, considerate, and lovable daughter. I am very proud of her.

Keith or Kouakou is my youngest son. He shows a pro-black, rebel spirit that he must pair with more career or skill-training in order for his rebel disposition to serve him well. Keith asked me to give him an African name, and after searching out a source of African names, I gave him the name "Kouakou," and he added "Boud Jiho-Bey." With his beard, his dread-locks, and his pro-black mindfulness, I believe that in time he will wear his African name nobly and wisely. I am proud of Kouakou because as a single parent he worked hard and long to take care of his two children. At this writing, KouaKou is still seeking-out his "best fit" in the world of work. His talents may be leading him toward becoming a rapper or music producer or a musical de-jay of note. I'll have to wait and see.

Miriam Greta Lewis is my step-daughter, my wife Sadie's daughter. I've come to love and think of her as one of my own children. Greta is smart, personable, and professional. She's what I call a "go-getter" and a good role model for all professional women. I am proud to call her my daughter.

Revisiting my son, Kevin: Kevin died during the time I was re-writing this book. I will share a part of his obituary with you.

"Lieutenant Colonel Kevin Timothy Bell, Sr. (Retired, USAF), age 60, died October 3, 2020. Kevin was born in Germany, raised in France, Ethiopia, and the eastern-seaboard of America. He eventually went to high school in Portsmouth, Virginia where he became a Manor High School honors graduate, and a member of the wrestling and cross-country teams. Kevin received an academic scholarship to Boston University, where he became a member of the wrestling team and earned a Bachelor's degree in Psychology. Two years later he earned his Master's degree in Social Work from Norfolk State University, and then completed Basic Officer Training School and receiving a commission as an Air Force Officer.

Lieutenant Kevin Bell began an outstanding 20 year career in the United States Air Force where he acquired numerous military decorations and citations. He retired from the Air Force in 2007, but continued working with the Military Behavioral Health Agency.

Kevin's laugh was infectious and brightened the spirits of those round him. His leadership, and his knowledge of social work were infinite, and he cared about and valued everyone he encountered."

I am proud of my son Kevin.

17.0 ON ROMANTIC LOVE AND MARRIAGE

17.10 ON ROMANTIC LOVE:

At this writing, I am "in love" with my wife Sadie and I have been in love with her for over 31 years. But what are these feelings we humans call love, "romantic love?" At best, I find it easier to speak about romantic love in a poem or a song, and I have done so below. I have purposely left the poem unfinished so that you might contemplatively complete it for yourself and to your own liking.

The feelings we call love
Love can be a hurting or a healing
That no one can really explain
The poets have best described it
As the ultimate pleasurable pain

Sometimes love tries to give
And sometimes it tries to take
Sometimes love rushes to repair
And sometimes it vows to break

Sometimes love will grow
And sometimes it self-destructs
Sometimes love will truly share
And sometimes it's selfish and corrupt

The feelings that we call love
From person to person will vary
To some it may be beautiful
And to others it can be scary

The feelings that we call love . . .

17.20 ON MARRIAGE:

I have married three times and divorced twice. At each marriage, I confessed to my bride that I loved her and at that time that confession was true. And so my marriage record does not qualify me to speak as an authority on marriage or does it? I once read a book about "Staying Happily Married" that had been written by a female marriage counselor, a PhD, who had married and divorced three times before she wrote the book. I assure you that there are many people who are living together or who have lived together for years as husband and wife and they are not comfortably or happily married. Outsiders may think of such couples as having a successful marriage, but outsiders never know. A long marriage does not indicate that the married people are "in love" or were ever "in love" or are still "in love." It only means they were married to each other for a long time and have "maintained." Nevertheless, we must note that to have "maintained" must be ruled "a plus" by outsiders.

18.0 MY PHILOSOPHICAL OUTLOOK

18.10 WHAT DO I KNOW ABOUT GOD?

To me, the word "God" is used to "give a personality" to the unfathomable life forces of the natural world. When I think "God," I am thinking "nature" or the "super-human" life creating, life sustaining, and life altering forces, substances, and dynamisms of the natural world. These life creating, life sustaining and life altering forces (God forces) are beyond the control and understanding of men. These forces are what they are; unfathomable, super-human, and natural! I do not believe these life altering forces are guided, driven, directed, or otherwise controlled by gods, goddesses, angels, jinns, demons, devils, or messiahs.

On the matter of our present day religions . . . all of them have been the primary cause of many wars since they have existed. These various religions had proclaimed "peace" or "peace on earth," but instead of being social instruments that promoted peace on earth, these religions have been social instruments that promote the separation of people into exclusive groups of "them" and "us." Nevertheless, different religions will always be a part of the social fabric of human societies. This means that if humans are to make a gain in establishing societies where law, justice, orderliness, and peace are to reside they must be able to coalesce around and be guided by humanistic principles.

I believe that all of the so-called "religious Holy Books" are creations of men; men who had an agenda, supposedly for the good of their societies, but often intended to control the thinking and behavior of the masses.

It is my steadfast conclusion that today in the 21st century, black men in America must rid themselves of the myths and allegories that lead to both Jesus worshipping and Islamic worship protocols. Further, it is my conclusion that black people must learn to present themselves as free-thinkers, humanists, and secularists if they are to become people of character and influence, and gain authentic self-respect.

18.20 AND WHAT DO I SAY ABOUT WORSHIP?

Do we all worship or venerate something or recognize something as "sacred"? Yes, I think we do. However, some of us haven't identified exactly what it is that we venerate or hold sacred or what we view with the greatest degree of appreciation and gratitude. For me, "the sacred" are the human life creating and sustaining forces of this earth. I may manifest my veneration simply by allowing myself a moment of silent meditation or reflection on something that has given me a good feeling or a feeling of wholeness and warmth. With me, these moments of veneration may be induced by the changing colors of leaves in autumn, or by watching children at play, or by recognizing that my grandchild has made a new discovery in his small but expanding world. All these small things allow me to momentarily pause and appreciate my ownership of this marvelous gift of consciousness that we call life.

18.30 MAN'S DESTINY:

Whatever happens to man on earth is not dependent on a God-character as depicted in the Bible or Quran or any other so-called holy book. Whatever happens to man is dependent on the superhuman forces of the natural universe and man's own character; his mutual caring and sharing, his logic and reasoning, and his actions. And as quiet as it may be kept this has always been the case.

The details of my arrival at the above philosophical views are noted in Appendix D.

19.00 My African Name

I have given myself an African name. My African name is Kwasi Ankoanna Asante. Kwasi means I was born on the seventh day of the week (Sunday, May 7, 1933). Ankoanna signals that I am a restless warrior until the enemy is defeated. Asante refers to the Asante tribe in Ghana that I have adopted as my ancestral tribe.

Why do I give myself an African name? I've given myself an African name because:

a) the name psychologically fortifies me to commit to the missions I described in Bits and Pieces #20, and reminds me of the invisible man or consciousness dwelling inside of me that requires me to do all I can with respect to these missions;

b) the name symbolically provides me a connection to my African ancestors, no matter how lowly they might have been, and symbolically rids me of the slave-master's familial name;

c) Once I am known by this name, the name will alert all persons (family, friends, and potential foes) that I am no longer an interested observer of black people's deleterious Jesus worshipping practices and white people's various masquerades of racism, but that now I am an activist who will aggressively campaign against these cultural and societal themes that prevent black people from becoming the best they might become.

My African name is simply my gift to myself; a gift that fulfills my personal need to self-identify, if to nobody but myself. And so, from this time forward you may call me "Chris" or "Kwasi" or simply "Ankoanna." I will answer to either of these names. And if you are so inclined, you may still call me "Junie."

20.0 MY PRESENT MISSIONS

My self-appointed missions since I retired from the US Department of Education are: (a) to help white and black people expand or extend their social and emotional comfort zones toward each other, and (b) to help rescue black (my) people from their deleterious Jesus worshipping practices.

The remainder of this Bits and Pieces will address the psychological and sociological stage on which I must work and a brief description of the work I am committed to do.

20.10 THE PSYCHOLOGICAL/SOCIOLOGICAL STATE OF BLACK AMERICANS (1996-2023):

The National Urban League's 1996 Report on "The State of Black America" cited several challenges facing black Americans. These challenges were: stabilizing the Black family and reducing out of wedlock child-births; eliminating alcoholism and drug addiction; combating poverty/unemployment/under-employment; improving health-care and wider social security coverage; improving educational opportunities; reducing high school drop-outs; decreasing homicides, suicides and spousal abuse; mobilizing economic and business enterprises; gaining a sense of moral purpose; nurturing strong, astute leaders; diminishing despair and building hope; maintaining high moral standards, and eliminating negative media propaganda.

It is my assessment that we, black people, are still facing these same challenges in 2014. It is also my assessment that we (black people) are at risk of perpetual social and economic distress due to our ignorance, our poverty, our greed, our misguided worship, and white racism. It is also my observation that we (black people) control three of these five at risk factors; our ignorance, our greed, and our misguided worship practices and that black people must accept blame for their status in these areas and many of us continue to work diligently toward perpetuating our own social and economic distresses. It is my belief that I can help to ameliorate some of our self-imposed problems if I work at the tasks I've indicated above and elaborate on below.

20.20 MY MISSION; PART ONE: HELPING BLACK AND WHITE PEOPLE EXPAND THEIR SOCIAL AND EMOTIONAL COMFORT-ZONES TOWARD EACH OTHER:

I presently undertake this mission by facilitating the A.D.O.R.E. (ADORE) forum at the Davies Memorial Unitarian Universalist (UU) Church in Camp Springs, Maryland. ADORE is the acronym for the words "A Dialogue on Race and Ethnicity," (A.D.O.R.E). In the ADORE forum, we discuss race relations and the "American Way" with the aim of exploring our feelings on racial issues and learning more about ourselves and others.

This mission requires more than facilitating the ADORE forums. To tackle this mission means that I must attend other functions that will allow me the opportunity to teach and preach to whites and blacks alike, especially whites about the American acculturation processes that inevitably leads to white superiority syndrome conditioning and indoctrination instead of humanistic conditioning and indoctrination I must also take advantage of opportunities to keep white people mindful of how their own hypocrisies regarding their racism have lead them to disguise their racism as other things: voter suppression, governmental shutdowns, and presidential disrespect (toward President Obama), voter re-districting, law enforcement and judicial inequalities, etc. I look forward to this challenge, and I know that my small efforts and the efforts of many others will help to bring about a positive change in race relations in America.

20.30 MY MISSION, PART TWO: HELPING TO RESCUE BLACK PEOPLE FROM THEIR PSYCHOLOGICAL AND EMOTIONAL DELETERIOUS PRACTICE OF JESUS WORSHIPPING:

There is a difference between the mentality and emotional well-ness of Christians who think of themselves as "Jesus followers" and those Christians who think of themselves as a "Jesus worshippers." To be Jesus followers is to be just that and no more. However, to be a Jesus worshipper is to place "Jesus" in a domain that is beyond and above humanity; making Jesus a symbol of god-likeness. I argue and declare that such worship is idolatrous and self-oppressive to black people.

This part of my mission requires that I write, engage, speak to, and work primarily with black people and the black clergy to inform them as to why and how their Jesus worshipping practice: (a) is idol worship that is equivalent to white male worshipping, and (b) indoctrinates them with a white superiority syndrome (WSS) that is psychologically, emotionally, and socially harmful, and negatively affects their sense of self-worth, self-efficacy, and their functional civic skills to successfully cope in America's white supremacy culture.

There is heavy psychological and emotional lifting required by me and other humanism campaigners dedicated to this mission. This is because we, the campaigners, must be prepared to engage with the black preachers and prod them to begin teaching a "new" Christianity; a Christianity which emphasizes humanistic values and ensures that Jesus Christ is not worshipped but viewed as a human being and a Jewish prophet. The greatest obstacle to black people changing from Jesus worshipping protocol to a truly humanistic protocol is the black clergy. The black clergy benefits from the money and gifts of a multitude of black people who are Jesus worshippers. The black Clergy has been successful in "selling" Jesus worshipping to black people, especially to black females, and the selling has been profitable. We cannot expect the black clergy to ever change from the "selling" of Jesus worshipping unless the black clergy is able by other means to maintain the financial well-being and prestige that it now enjoys. Therefore, the task of convincing black people to forego "Jesus worshipping" and to accept humanistic teachings as the foundation of their religious thinking will be long and hard, but it can be done. As for me, I have already begun the task. I've written two books that I use as starting points for information for the all Christians. These books **"The Belief Factor and the White Superiority Syndrome"** and **"The Black Clergy's misguided Worship Leadership"** are noted in Appendix E.

20.40 MY MISSION, PART THREE: HELPING, ENCOURAGING, AND EDUCATING ALL PEOPLE, ESPECIALLY WHITE ANGLO-SAXON PROTESTANT (WASP) MALES, VIA MY WRITINGS, LECTURES, AND ACTIONS TO REGARD HUMANISM AS A MORAL AND ETHICAL PHILOSOPHY FOR LIVING THAT TEACHES THAT HUMAN BEINGS THAT HOW THEY TREAT EACH OTHER, AND THEIR DESTINY REST IN THEIR OWN HANDS AND NOT IN THE HANDS OF A SUPERHUMAN GOD WHO CONTROLS THEIR LIVES.

This mission proceeds toward several goals: (a) the elimination of religious idols, (b) the termination, elimination, and interruption of the transfer or acquisition of White Superiority Syndrome (WSS) conditioning agencies and factors that are prevalent around the world, and (c) the neutralization/elimination of institutional racism.

21.0 Concerning life, death, truth, friendships, and Law and Order

21.10 ON LIFE:

Life is this gift that I call "consciousness." This consciousness is a blessing; a blessing to always be appreciated and celebrated. None of us can explain it, but it is how we are able to discover ourselves and the world around us. The eternal question related to life is, "What is the best way for a person to use it, to live it, to show his/her appreciation for it, and to celebration it?" So-called wise men of past civilizations have suggested answers to this question, but ultimately the answer is a personal matter and each person must and eventually will answer it for himself.

For me, I wish to live life with fulfilling work and parenting, celebrate it with laughter, loving, and fellowshipping with like-minded people, and seek out my appreciation of it with contemplations or investigations of the grandeur and mysteries of the world of nature that surrounds me.

21.20 ON DEATH:

Everything on earth that now lives will die one day. This is a fundamental physical law of Nature that all of us must acknowledge. Death is unwelcomed by most of us, and like the rest of humanity, I must learn to deal with it in ways that are not self-destructive, self-depressing, or death-fearing. How does one do this? Since I've become an adult, the presents of death has always made me sorrowful, and like most people, I simply brace myself and do the best I can. However, I refuse to engage long with those who are sorrow-celebrating, and sorrow-loving personalities and who at every possible opportunity make themselves front-line witnesses to the sickness, dying, or funerals of others. As quiet as it may be kept, there are some people who gain an emotional high when they become front-line witnesses of life—to-death dramas, and they work hard at making the sorrowful ethos of such dramas last as long as possible. I am out of place is such company.

I am sorrowful when children and young people die, because most of them may not have gotten a chance to live a life where they could and did make choices. But it is Nature's plan that old people die, and as such their dying isn't a tragedy. It isn't a tragedy because old people (60 years plus) have had the opportunity to make choices in how to live; albeit that their choices may have been bad choices for them. I do not give reverence to the presence of death. I sorrowfully acknowledge death when it enters my domain, attend to the remains of the dead, and try hard to move on toward life's gifts of loving, laughter, work, and fellowship.

21.30 ON TRUTH:

The philosophical statement that says "Know the truth and the truth shall set you free" is a lie! "Knowing the truth" will never set you free. **To be free, one must have the courage to act or speak and face-off with those who would deny you your freedom.** Often, if not always, the powerful tend to declare what is considered to be the truth (their version) and the weak have no practical choice except to acquiesce. When acquiescence is not required, many people favor myths and make-belief as guideposts instead of the truth. This is because myths and make-belief are more emotionally satisfying and avoids a confrontation with the powers that control the status-quo. The truth about the "truth" is that in the normal dallying of life, it is only revealed or acknowledged as the last resort and then often grudgingly.

21.40 ON FRIENDSHIPS:

I can think of no greater spiritual, emotional, or psychological pleasure available to human beings than healthy and prospering children, personal health, warm and understanding fellowship and contacts, and loving personal relations.

21.50 ON LAW AND ORDER:

I have often heard our political leaders state how important it is that the general public must allow "law and order" to prevail or that "law and order" should be our civic motto for good government. It is my opinion that this motto is short-sighted in that it doesn't include the word "justice." The motto should be "Law, justice, and order." Within a society with a system of laws and no declaration of dedication to justice in the administration of those laws, the only order that will exit is the order imposed by the lawmakers and their friends. A society that allows unfair treatment in the application and administration of its laws is a society that must be continually alert for rebellion and riots from within its borders.

22.0 THE BOOKS I'VE WRITTEN: SEE APPENDIX F

23.00 MY OPTIMISTIC OUTLOOK ON AMERICA

I have a long range optimistic and inspiring outlook on the future of black people in America. But in order for my outlook to be realized, lots of work must be done to bring white and black people to the point of authentic mutual respect. Let me explain.

I have three focused outlooks. I have a present day focus (0 to 5 years), a short-range future focus (6-20 years), and a long-range optimistic future focus (20-40 years).

1. <u>Regarding my present day focus (0 to 5 years)</u>: When I look out today (in 2014), I see Americans engaged in a great "Cultural War" between its white supremacy cultural practices and a growing counter -culture that stresses the principles espoused in the American Declaration of Independence . Today , white racism is alive and vigorous , and it uses many disguises as it masquerades as other things. One of the primary racial problems is America in 2014 is the political dislike and distaste of many white males to the unanticipated and unbelievable reality of the existence of a black, American President, Barack Obama. Many white Americans males are still reacting angrily in their adjustment to the shock of a black man being elected as president of the United States. The election of a black man to the American Presidency was due in part young Americans and white women who were or had been dismayed by America 's unsuccessful and continuous engagements in two wars, a national financial and banking crisis, high and increasing unemployment among white middle-class, educated workers. Unfortunately, many educated and prosperous white males do not accept the thesis that black men may or should ever be in charge of white men, and these few, but powerful men are doing all they can to prevent the black president's plans and programs from succeeding.

   In addition to this nation-wide problem, there exists at many local and state levels many racial problems and dilemmas wherein white-rule and white-control are the norm and where racial justice and fairness are in short supply. The fight for racial justice and fairness is at its root a cultural war. Today, I am a warrior in this cultural war. I am on the side that works to bring white people to an awareness of their hypocrisies and their white privilege and to act as a prick to their conscious in a way that will prompt them to change.

2. <u>Regarding my short range future focus (6-20 years)</u>: From 6-20 years from now, I perceive that America will still be involved in a cultural war. But this is where my optimism kicks in. This is because:

   a) As history has shown and will show again and again, natural crisis, geo-political forces, and social challenges from both inside and outside of America's boundaries will force white and black Americans to expand their "comfort zones" toward each other so as to ensure their mutual survival, protection, and prosperity. Although this scenario foresees national crisis or urgencies as prods in helping to improve race relations, the end result will be a better and stronger and more equalitarian America.

   b) The rise, expansion, and acknowledgement of American women leadership will flourish. It is my belief that American female leadership in the major political, social, educational, and civic settings of America will be the "saving grace" with regards to overseeing the general welfare of the nation, including improving race relations. I see and sense that female leadership will bring racial justice much sooner to the American way of life than white male leadership is psychologically or emotionally able to do. American women, black and white, will rise up and become U.S. Presidents, Governors of States, Senators and Congress-people, business and financial executives, military leaders, college presidents, and worship leaders. Race relations in America will improve with American women leaders because of their superior survival and leadership skills and their humanistic valuing and temperaments.

3. <u>Regarding my long-range optimistic future focus (21-40 years)</u>: In the 21-40 year time period from now, time and events will have provided more and more Americans, blacks and whites, with experiences that will make them aware and conscious of the willingness to sacrifice their time and energy to promote racial fairness and social justice. This willingness to sacrifice will not come automatically. It will come by way of: the prodding of many little campaigners like me; the challenges of man-made problems and crisis from outside and inside American; and the threat or malevolence of natural forces or diseases. This willingness will take time, but it will come because the survival and upward progress of America and the human species will require that it materializes.

24.00 MY HEAVYWEIGHT REGRETS AND FEARS

Some of them I have already noted in this book, but I have others that I do not wish to share. Now at age 80 plus years, I can honestly say that I have forgiven myself with regard to most of these regrets and I have challenged myself not to repeat them.

I regret that early on, I gave very few white men the benefit of the doubt about them being non-racist or fair-minded when I first met them. This means I probably lost good white men who would-have been strong allies.

I regret that I have not yet convinced many black people, including some family members, that "Jesus worshiping" is equivalent to "white male worshiping." This means that although I did my best, I may not have gathered together the best series of words to weave into strong sentences, that speak thought-provokingly to Black people in a way to convince them that they must worship only God, their Creator, and stop their idolatrous "Jesus Worshiping" practices. Gathering the psychological strength to eliminating Jesus worship from his alignment with the universe is the Black man's key burden to realizing and authenticating his own first-class humanity. Until the black man realizes that "Jesus worship" is idolatrous "white male worship", the black man will never be able in the depths of his psychic truly believe himself to be equal to white men.

I fear that what I write or say with regard to my missions (Section 20.20) have and will fall on many unhearing ears and un-ready minds and much of my efforts in this matter will not bring an end to "Jesus worshipping." Never-the-less, I am compelled to speak my truth as I see and feel it. And so, I must HOPE that somehow, somewhere, and in some way there are many other humanists who are also campaigning on these same matters, and that inch-by-inch, the world will be transformed into millions of neighborhoods of humanists.

I fear that the tasks of eliminating white superiority syndrome (wss) conditioning factors and institutionalized racism from the American psychic will never be fully completed. Such tasks are really the Black man's burden. The Black clergy would be the key black operators to commit themselves to these tasks, but the Black clergy has shown little interest in the matter. As long as white superiority syndrome (wss) conditioning factors prevail in America and both black and white people participate in Jesus worshiping, the Black man will never gain the psychological freedom of authentic self-respect and gain racial justice, equality, and liberty.

25.00 SOME OF MY FAVORITES FOR RELAXING AND MEDITATING

25.10 POEMS:

If (Kipling); When Malindy Sings, The Colored Soldiers (Dunbar); A Psalm of Life, The Arrow and the Song (Longfellow); Once upon a Sidewalk Café, It's an Inside job, Promise Yourself (Bell); The Blind men and the Elephant (Saxe);

25.20 SONGS:

Old Man River; You are My Sunshine; Come Sing a Song with me; That's Life; Imagine; Let it Be a Dance; My Way; Stormy Weather; Autumn Leaves; To Beat the Devil; The Sunflower Song; I hope you dance; Je ne regrette rien;

Quranic surahs: 3:64-68, 5:72-77, and 112
Bible verses: Isaiah 40:28-31; Mark 12: 29-34; Matt 21: 42-44;

26.00 WRAP-UP/WARM-UP

This section is where I wrap-up my first 80 plus years and begin warming-up for my next 80 plus years.

26.10: MY PERSONAL CREST:

In 1962, Monsieur Paul Lussan, who worked with me when I was assigned to the U.S. Army Donges Petroleum Terminal near St. Nazaire, France, designed and presented me with a personal crest as a farewell gift. M. Lussan was a noted designer of official "Coat of Arms" for several French cities (villages) in the Bretagne Province of north-west, France.

M. Lussan designed the Crest based on my name and zodiac sign. I wished he had asked me in advance so that I could have made him aware that his design should have some reference to my African origins and American slavery heritage. But an unexpected gift is a gift, and I appreciated his friendship and consideration.

26.20: FUTURE PLANS:

I intend to continue to study, write, and fellowship in the same ways I have done during the last twenty (20) years. This plate of activities should keep me hopeful in providing insight to others in bettering race relationships, and instrumental in spurring a black intellectual awakening regarding their own self-worth. I shall attempt to use the Boy Scout Laws as the core of my "prime directive" in relating to other humans. I shall continue to spread the intellectual and moral seeds of humanism with the hope that we humans learn to respect each other as we would wish to be respected.

APPENDICES

APPENDIX A:
A SNAPSHOT OF MY MOTHER;
OLIVIA WILLIAMS BELL

My mother, Olivia Williams Bell was born March 27, 1914 in Roanoke, Alabama, the daughter of Daniel (Dee) Williams and Carrie Bell Williams. My mother was three years old when her parents came to Norfolk where she spent the rest of her life. She died December 21, 1944.

As I now remember Mama Olivia, she was plump and short. She showed me how to read and sing the lyric lines on a song-sheet. I remember us singing Red River Valley, You are my Sunshine, My Blue Heaven, We Three Kings,(Christmas song), and Silent Night. There were other songs, but I don't remember their titles.

Mama Olivia listened to radio soap-opera programs of Just Plain Bill, Ma Perkins, As the World Turns, and others. Sometimes she listened with me to radio programs such, as Superman, Jack Armstrong, the Green Hornet, The Shadow, Mister District Attorney, and the Cisco Kid.

Mama Olivia cooked over a wood-burning stove. I remember on several occasions when the weather was bad, she cooked sweet-potato biscuits for me and Madeline, and the house would be filled with the aroma of these biscuits cooking. I remember how Madeline and I would butter the biscuits and slowly eat them, trying to make them last a long time.

Mama Olivia maintained a scrapbook in which she wrote down her thoughts or kept pictures and newspaper clippings. Some of her scrapbook writings are included in this appendix.

MY OTHER REMEMBRANCES:

When I was between 8-10 years old and would be out playing somewhere in the neighborhood and Mama wanted me, she'd come to the front or back door (depending on the direction she thought I would be) and she would call out as loud as she could, "Juuunie! Juuunie Bell!" Sometimes I didn't hear her because I would be playing with cars underneath somebody's house or I'd be playing down in the "marsh," (see note below) behind Covel Street. When I heard her calling, I would run home to see what she wanted. Seems that most of the time when she called me, she just wanted to make sure I was still within calling distance.

Note: The marsh was a low, sea-weeded wetland area that was the end-point of a muddy tributary from the Elizabeth River. The marsh was one of our play areas. We played soldiers (American against Germans), and cowboy and Indians there. In the marsh, we often found terrapins and frogs, and we saw rabbits, squirrels, and sometime snakes. There were also a few clusters of blackberry and strawberry bushes, along with wild peach and cherry trees.

WRITINGS OF MAMA OLIVIA (AS THEY APPEAR IN HER SCRAPBOOK)

MY BOY

He goes out and stays all day
He won't come home to eat
He never gets hungry
As long as he's in the street

I go to the door and call him
Junior don't you ever want to eat
But he's perfectly happy
As long as he's out in the street

My Boy has plenty things
To keep him out of doors
No matter how rough he plays
He's not rough on his clothes

At home he plays being Tarzan
A chair becomes his tree
And under the table his Jungle
He pictures animals in his memory

He loves playing out of doors
To me he is a real boy
And when he grows into a man
To me I hope he'll bring great joy

TWIN BEDS?

I, Olivia Williams Bell, was born in Roanoke Alabama in the year of Our Lord 1914. I came to Virginia in 1917 and have resided here every since.

As a child, I was not content. I had a mind to travel and never settle down. And if ever I married, I didn't want any children. And my husband and I should have twin beds.

I was married at the age of seventeen to Christopher Cleophus Bell, my husband still, and he made me change my mind about twin beds. And I have two fine children at this writing. I would not sleep in a twin bed now if I had one. And as for children, I would not take a million dollar for either of them.

As for contentment, I have found it one of the best things in life. I don't want to travel now because I have nothing to seek for. When you find the one person you can feel secure with, you will be content. It makes no difference whether you live in a palace or a log cabin you will be happy.

GIVE ME FLOWERS NOW (JANUARY 1940)

Have you ever notice when somebody dies
No matter what he is or what he has been
A saintly person, or one who's
Life has been steep in sin
His friends forget the bad
That was done yesterday
And think of all fine
And pretty words to say
Perhaps when I go to rest

Someone will bring to light

Some kind deed or some good thought,

Long buried out of sight.

But if it's all the same to you,

Please give to me instead,

The flower while I am living

And the knocking when I am dead

Don't save them to put upon my grave

While now you are throwing stones at me

From every hiding place

Some of the stones are heavy

Some of them are light

Some you throw in the day time

And some you throw at night

Say some kind word to me

While I live here below

Because I can't hear anything you say

When I reach that other show

What will I know when I am dead?

It won't flatter me no matter what is said.

So please give me the flowers now

And not when I am dead

MY HUSBAND (JANUARY 1940)

My husband is a faithful man
Every day he does his duty,
Building up things around our house
Giving it new life and beauty
He's built another room onto our house
He said that he could do it
He took his hammer, nails, and saw
And started to work on it
Now the room he has finished
He has labored long and hard
I can praise him but not enough
For God gives all a just reward

APPENDIX B:

A SNAPSHOT OF MY FATHER, CHRISTOPHER C. BELL SR.:

Christopher Cleophus Bell Sr., my dad, was born in Norfolk County, Virginia, June 26, 1909, the son of Alexina Mullen Bell and William Henry Bell, and he died August 30, 1973.

Daddy lived in Norfolk all his life and had been active in the church almost all his life. Daddy had been Chairman of the Deacon Board, a member of the Finance Committee, member of the Male Chorus. Previous to these tasks, he had been a church school teacher, a Vacation Bible School leader, a tither, and a Sunday school superintendent.

Dad's civic and community affiliations included: Past Master of Ebenezer Lodge #66 AF & AM Masons, Past Patron of Eastern Star, Elizabeth Chapter #34, Institutional Representative of the Boy Scouts of America, Member of the NAACP, and Vice-President of the Campostella Civic League.

When my Mama Olivia died, my Dad had to care for and raise me and my five sisters. My dad was a mailman. He went to work wearing a uniform, came home, cooked, and washed clothes as necessary. Madeline (Mat, my older sister) and I could take care of ourselves, but we had to help Dad care for our younger sisters; Olivia, Lillie, Martha, and Jessie. Madeline and I helped in every way. For about a year, Dad paid a helper to come over each school day morning to help us to get my younger sisters bathed and dressed and to fix breakfast for them because Madeline and I had to get ready and go to school.

Daddy gave me plenty of slack in going and coming as long as I did my chores, but he was a stern task-master to Madeline. He often made her stay home when some of her girl-friends were playing or socializing. I remember telling him that he should let her have more fun with her friends, but he didn't change.

We were a church-going family. Dad made us (his children) go to church school every Sunday or we couldn't go any other place that day.

Dad didn't smoke. He didn't curse either, except for one time when he accidentally hit his finger with a hammer while driving a nail into a 2 by 4 piece of lumber. He worked hard around the house. He knew how to handle a horse and plow too. He plowed the fields around our house and he and I planted sweet potatoes, lima beans, and collards. All of us (my sisters) helped with the gathering and picking of the ripened vegetables.

Dad built an extension to our house. He added a bathroom and two bedrooms. By the way, we didn't have indoor plumbing until I was twelve or thirteen. We got electricity when I was six years old, but we didn't get paved streets until after I was seventeen or eighteen years old. I worked as my Dad's helper when he worked on the house. He did the carpentry, wall work, and brick work. I helped dig the holes for the extension foundation and when Dad laid the bricks, I was the brick-boy. When he put up the plaster wall-boards, I helped to lift and hold them in place so he could nail them together. The hardest part of this work was to place these heavy wallboards on the ceiling. I stood on the ladder and held the wallboards with my head and hands and he got on another ladder and started nailing. My Dad was a carpenter, a brick layer, a cook, and a farmer. I don't know how he learned all these skills, but I watched him as he literally expanded our house to twice its original size; and I helped.

Six or seven months after becoming a boy scout(at 12 years old), I acquired a Boy Scout guide-book, two merit badge manuals, a First Aid guide-book, a European history book, a Greek mythology book, and a Seamanship's Guide manual from my uncle, **Welton Williams**, who was a Merchant Marine. My dad saw these books in a corner of our house on the floor, and he said "Junior, you need some place to keep these books. Let's do you a book-case." In a week or so, he got the type wood he wanted. He measured and marked in pencil where he wanted me to saw (cut) the wood, and when I finished sawing (cutting), he did the nailing. We built a bookcase; about 6 ft. tall, 24" wide, and 10" deep that had four or five shelves. When the bookcase stood by itself, he told me to sand it down. He showed me how to put on the first and second coat of varnish and make the wood shine. Dad placed the book case in our living room and told me that all of us would use it. That was fine by me. I think this bookcase is still in my sister Lillie's home.

When Dad died, he was so well liked by his church that the church leaders established the **"Christopher Bell Brotherhood League";** a church organization dedicated to improving church related male-fellowship and sponsoring events to help fund other church programs. Dad left a notebook in which he had outlined the story for a novel and had written a few poems. Two of his poems are noted below.

PICK ME OUT OF THE AIR (1925)

Address:
Planet: The Earth
World: New World
Hemisphere: Western
Continent: North America
Country: United States
State: Virginia
Section: Tidewater
County: Norfolk
Vicinity: Campostella
Street: Pike
Number: 328
Family: Bell
Sex: Male
Name: Christopher C
Got Me?

Work! (1929)
The workman awakes
His dreams he brakes
And sits on his bed a-yarning
The ground was white
From the frost that night
And the day was just a-dawning

Some workmen go
Down to the sea
And some to fields a-winding
Some workers go
Into their workshops
Or into the mountain a-mining

Others enter mills
And with an honest will
For them work can be fun
They'll work their way
Through the day
Till the old west welcomes the sun

For a bird to rest
There must be a nest
And for a fox, a den
For the world
To keep going around
It must have its working men

The workers labor
In winter and fall
As chilly winds are blowing
And in the spring and summer
They're up with the birds
Where forests and flowers are growing

My Dad's poems have rough edges, but I think they're great! He also wrote and delivered several speeches which I think are also wonderful.

My Dad had a habit of singing songs in a raspy, almost hoarse tone as he moved around the house. Sometimes it was hard to make-out what he was singing, but eventually the tune came into focus. Several of his favorite raspy songs were Old Man River, Water Boy, Danny Boy, and Just a Closer Walk with Thee. There were many others but I don't remember them.

Appendix C:

A SNAPSHOT OF MAMA ELSIE:

My Mama Elsie was born Elsie Virginia Armstrong, November 12, 1912 in Princess Anne County, Virginia. She was the daughter of Earnest and Daisy Armstrong. Mama Elsie died April 29, 2012 in Smithfield, Virginia.

When Dad married Mama Elsie, I was 13 years old and a freshman in high school. I was pretty much independent and had lots of outside-the-home interests. This meant that Mama Elsie and I didn't spend time getting to know each other as mother and son. Nevertheless, I knew Mama liked me from the start because of the warm consideration she gave me, and I returned her considerations with politeness and spontaneous assistance whenever I saw a chance to do so. I felt that Mama Elsie was extremely helpful to Dad in taking care of my younger sisters and keeping things at home smooth and easy-going. In every way I could I tried to show her that I really appreciated her as a mother.

I don't recall a single incident or event in which Mama Elsie expressed disfavor with anything I had done. I do know that (in my child's mind) Mama Elsie was a "good-looking" lady and my Dad was lucky to have married her, and I was determined to make her feel proud of the fact that she had married him. I saw Mama Elsie as a blessing to Dad, to me and to my sisters in many ways. So whenever she would ask me to do something, I would do it quickly.

I remember one night I was studying at our dining room table and Mama Elsie placed a slice of pie or cake on the table beside my books and said, "Try this, junior. I cooked it today. Let me know how you like it." It was simple acts like this one that registered in my mind about the goodness of Mama Elsie. By the way, the cake or pie was good and I told her so.

For years, Mama Elsie was very active in church until she had a stroke and had to discontinue her services. She had been a past Chairman of the Deaconess Board, a Member of: the Workers for Christ, the Pastor's Aide Society, the Eastern Star (Elizabeth Chapter #34), and the Salvation Army. She was the founder of the Garland G. Pretlow Senior Citizens Club in Campostella.

APPENDIX D:

MY SPIRITUAL/RELIGIOUS JOURNEYING:

1. **My childhood memories of church and God**: I grew up in what would now be called a fundamentalist Baptist household. In our dining room, there was a picture of a "Praying Jesus in the Garden of Gethsemane," who was blond with White European features. In the picture Jesus' face was illuminated by a ray of light coming down from the sky. My Dad required us, my sisters and me, to go to Sunday school every Sunday. If we didn't go to Sunday school, he would not allow us to go anywhere else on Sunday. So ours was a strict church-going household.

   My earliest imaginings of God was that God was a large, bearded, White man with a stern visage and piercing blue eyes and that he sat on a kingly gold and silver throne just beyond the blue sky or behind the clouds, and that he wore a purple or a white, gold-trimmed robe.

2. **My first religious questionings:** When I was eleven years old and my mother was hit and killed by an automobile, I began questioning God. My mother (Mama Olivia) was hit by a car on Dec 20, 1944 as she rushed across Wilson Road to catch a bus on her way to Christmas shopping. She died Dec 21, 1944 and we had her funeral on Christmas Eve, December 24, 1944. On Christmas Eve night, my older sister, Marjorie (Mat), and I helped my Dad play Santa Clause to our four younger sisters, Olivia, Lilly, Martha, and Jessie.

   Before Mama Olivia's death, I had not given much thought to what was taught in Sunday school, but I had learned that when good people died, they went to heaven and when bad people died they went to hell. I do remember that I didn't grieve outwardly about my mother's death as did my sister Mat and the adults in the family. Perhaps this was because I was convinced that I could be a good boy and be so good that God would reward me by returning my mother to me. This meant that I had to learn what specifically I would have to do to get God to return my mother.

3. **Searching for God:** I started searching for God by reading selected parts of the Bible, especially from the New Testament. I was a good reader and I wanted to get to know about

God and give God a chance to "know me" and then give him a chance to give my mother back to me. In my effort to convince God that he should return my mother, I joined the church. At 12 years old I got baptized, and became a very good and proper boy. I did my chores. I lived my Boy Scout Laws. I became a star pupil in school. By 14 years of age, I had become the teacher of the Adult Church School class, and often I was called on to review the Sunday school lesson in front of the whole Sunday school assembly. Most of the people in the church believed that I was going to be a young, powerful, Baptist preacher, and maybe I did too.

4. **My God-searching results:** In the high school library, I took out books on religion. Some of these books did not feature the Bible or Christianity and I read them too. At about 14 years of age, my patience with God ran out. God had not returned my mother, and from my adolescent awakening to the real world and formal (logical) thinking, as well as my readings, I knew that God could not return my mother. I knew this because reasoning even for an adolescent point of view allowed me to realize that there really was no God, at least there was no God as described in the Bible. I think I knew this even before I got into the readings. I guess the readings just confirmed what my pre-teenage mind was telling me at the start; that all religions were mostly based on myths and superstitions. Now I knew from my readings that "God" was a word used to personalize the power and forces of nature; to give nature and its mysteries a personality and allow men to think about them as if they were a superior being that could relate to humans. My readings also confirmed for me that all religions (the ancient Egyptians religions, Islam, Mithraism, Hinduism, and Zoroastrism, Christianity) were myths and allegories designed to inspire the imaginations, fears, hopes, and ambitions of a culture or society.

5. **Challenging my father:** One Sunday, at 14 years of age, after I had done most of my cross-cultural religious readings, I decided not to go to church. My sister Olivia asked me why I wasn't going. I simply told her that I just wasn't going. Olivia ran and told my Dad what I had said. My Dad, who was the Church School superintendent at that time, came into my little bedroom and asked, "What is your problem, boy?" I remember looking him in the eyes and saying, "Daddy, God didn't make man in his image. Men made God in their image." For a long moment my Dad looked questioningly at me, and then while keeping his eyes on me, he backed out of my room and closed the door. A few moments later, I heard my sister Olivia asking him if I would now be going to church. I heard my Dad say, "Leave him alone. He's going to be all right."

I didn't go to church that Sunday and I also went out visiting with my friends later that day. From that day on, my Dad did not pressure me to go to Sunday school or church. I went to church off and on, just enough to keep our neighbors thinking that my father was overseeing a God-fearing home.

6. **Moving from religion to philosophy:** From age 15 until I was a father raising my own children, I let religion go its way and I went mine. In college at age 17, I discovered the word "agnostic," and that is what I called myself. I regarded the Bible as a book of fiction with a few factual historical events thrown in. My personal "Prime Directive" was "To try to treat others as I would want to be treated by them and try to live according to the "Boy Scout Law" (See note below). As you might suspect, I didn't always stay true to my "Prime Directive" or the Boy Scout Law, but neither the promise of heaven's gifts or of hell's punishments directed or guided my actions and thinking.

Note: The Boy Scout law is; "A Scout is trustworthy, loyal, helpful, friendly, courteous, kind, obedient, cheerful, thrifty, brave, clean, and reverent"

When I was in the military, I began taking my children to Sunday school (at the military chapel on the army post) when my youngest (of three) became three years old. I felt that in Church school they would learn that if they were good children good things would happen to them. Now as I look back, this philosophical stance didn't hurt me or my children. They learned the need (moral imperative) to first respect themselves and then to respect others.

The psychological reality of white superiority syndrome (WSS) conditioning: While I was in the military, religion was not a consideration to me in any form. However, when I attended graduate school in Cambridge and Boston (1974-1978), the professors of education were debating the causes of the "academic achievement gap." Educational testing results since the beginning of school integration had shown that black adolescents scored significantly lower than white adolescents on standardized academic achievement tests. What were the causes of this gap: intelligence difference; Home life (parental education) difference; environmental or cultural difference? These discussions prompted me to search for answers to this "gap problem" question. Beyond anything that the professors might teach or write, my review and analysis of my own life told me that this "gap problem" had nothing to do with black adolescents' genes or intellectual abilities.

Many years after graduate school, I continued to read and reason on the question of the academic achievement gap. After several years of civilian work experiences, my self-analysis, intuition, observations, and my reasoning led me to conclude that the academic achievement "gap" between black and white adolescents was, in part, a normal result of black children becoming conditioned and indoctrinated toward acquiring a white superiority syndrome (wss) as a result of their long term and sustained exposure to white-male supremacy acculturation. I reasoned that by the time black children became adolescents, the prevailing American white male supremacy cultural ethos negatively affected their self-esteem and disillusioned them with regard to their post-school livelihood and thus their academic motivation was suppressed and the "gap" appeared. I reasoned that black children were being subliminally conditioned by the white supremacy culture of America to feel inferior to white people and their low testing scores was an indicator of this conditioning.

In my writings, I have referred to this American white supremacy ethos and its conditioning effects as white superiority syndrome (WSS) conditioning and indoctrination. But more than this, I also reasoned that Christianity with its Jesus worshipping protocol was one of these WSS conditioning and indoctrination factors. My logic and my intuition told me that worshipping Jesus Christ, who is portrayed as a white male and celebrated as the Son of God is idol worship and the equivalent of white male worshipping. I also concluded that such a worship protocol will always prevent black men from ever feeling or thinking of themselves as being equal to white men.

7. **Giving Christianity another look**: I decided to investigate whether there was a redeeming element within Christianity itself that would serve to neutralized the deleterious effects of Jesus worshipping on black people, and so I enrolled in a conservative Christian Bible college.

My first class was a course entitled: A Survey of the Old Testament. In the first fifteen minutes of the class, the professor stated that the physical world was about 7000-8000 years old, based on the calculations of the generations and years of life of the people noted in the Bible from Adam and Eve until now (1989). From that point on, my studies at the college were unfulfilling. Most, if not all of the allegories were treated as if they were factual events: i.e.; a talking serpent; a God who comes to walk with Adam; two different versions of the creation story; the two versions of the unbelievable Noah story; the completely irrational story of Jonah in the belly of a fish for three days; the allegory of Abraham, Sarah, Hagar, Isaac and Ismail.

I knew after this first class meeting that I would never be a Baptist preacher because I would not be able to bring my intellectual honesty to bear if I treated the Old Testament as if it were fact. I and everybody in that class knew that the Old Testament was primarily a book of myths, allegories, and fictional stories, but nobody spoke up and disputed the professor. I completed this course and enrolled for the following semester in a course entitled; A Survey of the New Testament. Again the same professor taught the myths, allegories, and fictional stories of the Bible as if they were historical facts. I was more certain than ever that the "Jesus worship" protocol endorsed by Christianity and practiced by black people was not only idolatrous, but that for black people, Jesus worship was self-demeaning, psychologically oppressive, and promoted a white superiority syndrome (WSS) conditioning into their sense of reality.

8. **Giving Islam a first look:** Several years after my Bible College experience, I investigated Islam within the framework of the American Muslim Association movement.

   Note: American Muslim Association is primarily a black group of Islamic believers who are organized under the stewardship of Imam Wallace D. Mohammah, whose father was Elijah Mohammah, the founder of the Nation of Islam in America.

I knew that Islam rejected the idea of "Jesus worshipping" and viewed Jesus as a Jewish prophet, a human being and a messenger from God (Allah). This theology satisfied me to the extent that it got rid of "Jesus worshipping," but I became dismayed with Islam as I studied and experienced it. A few of my reasons for dismay are noted below.

   a) American Muslims often adopted Arab dress and this practice unnecessarily increased their separateness from other Americans, black as well as white. In my opinion this unnecessary practice diminished Muslim progressiveness in building multicultural and inter-community relationships;

   b) Male sexism was flagrantly practiced and this practice violated my sense of social justice and egalitarianism between men and women;

   c) Islam did nothing to curb white racism in Arab-Muslim countries with regard to how black people are treated. Racism was as evident in Saudi Arabia when I visited there as it is in America. Perhaps it is not widely known by most black American Muslims that the Arabs began enslaving black Africans long before the Europeans began such enslavement, and their treatment of their African slaves was just as brutal as that of the Europeans.

   d) Black American Muslims often gave themselves Arab-names. I considered this Arab-name change to be what some writers have described as an act of "Self-Inferiorization." Self-Inferiorization is a pattern of individual and/or collective behaviors that reflect or show low self-esteem, self-denigration, or acts against one's own self-interest, and a willing acceptance of un-redeeming, demeaning social and anti-social roles.

It is my thinking that when American black people give themselves Arab names, they glorify Arab culture, and by so doing, they lose their own "Africa to America to Freedom pilgrimage" story; and thus they isolate themselves from their own real-life heritage. It is my opinion that if black Muslims must have a name-change they should embrace their own history by adopting West-African names; thus avoiding cultural self-inferiorization.

e) Islam by my readings and observations is a political system as well as a religion. I believe in the separation of government/politics from religion, and so I am at odds with any thinking that would have religious dogma trump logic and reason in determining the secular welfare of the society.

Given the dismays noted above about Islam and also other observations which I care not to mention, I 've concluded that the only cultural and sociological advantage of Islam over Christianity to black people in America is that blacks who become Muslims have theoretically escaped from the deleterious effects of "Jesus worshipping." However, by becoming Muslims, they have placed themselves in the self-inferiorization role of mimicking Arabs; a role that prevents them from ever learning to realize their own true human potential.

Before I formally left the American Muslim Movement, I worked with two Muslim brothers who were United States Army veterans **(Brother Mujhaid Muhammad and Brother Taalib Din Abdul-Wakil)** and together we founded and organized (1997) the **Muslim American Veterans Association (MAVA). The MAVA is a secular, veteran and community service organization.** I served as its first president (Commander) at Post 1, located in Washington DC. At this writing (2014), the MAVA is recognized by the Veteran Administration as an authentic, national, veteran organization. MAVA has established "posts" in at least six (6) major cities in the United States.

9. **Finding Unitarian Universalism (U.U.):** In 1997, I visited Davies Memorial U.U. Church in Camp Springs, Maryland. I was attracted to this church because of its newspaper advertisement. The advertisement read: "Course Offering; 'Building Your Own Theology. . .'" I wanted to see what kind of church was brave enough to advertise this type of course and so I ventured out to see them. After my first visit and discussion with the members of the "Building Your own Theology" class, I knew that I could find a comfortable "spiritual

and intellectual fit" for my humanistic values in the Unitarian Universalist (UU) church community, and I have done just that.

Unitarians like most people are a group of men and women who stretch themselves to be better people, but they try to do so with the least amount of myths and superstitions to guide their way. Most of the Unitarians I have met are white secular humanists. Most of them, like many other white people, have had little fellowship with black people. However, my experience has lead me to feel that most of them are consciously attempting to move forward at improving race relations by all rational means available to them. Their good-will efforts and their fellowship with me have served to inspire me to move forward with regards to my personal missions I described in Bits and Pieces #20.

10. **The glory and purity of simplicity:** I am honestly compelled to admit that, to date, in all my inquiries into religions and philosophies of living, I have found no better formula for life guidance among humans than the twelve principles of the Boy Scout Law, which I learned when I was 11 years old. **The Boy Scout Law simply states: a scout is trustworthy, loyal, helpful, friendly, courteous, kind, obedient, cheerful, thrifty, brave, clean, and reverent. I can honestly say that there is nothing in any of all the religions that can top these guiding principles.**

11. One of the truths that I've become aware of during my spiritual wanderings, and reflections is the following:

To be White and accept consciously or unconsciously the image of God as a white male is the greatest example of White Superiority Syndrome (WSS) conditioning that leads to white supremacist thinking and institutional racism,

and

To be Black and accept consciously or unconsciously the image of God as a white male is a grand example of White Superiority Syndrome (WSS) conditioning that leads to self-negations and diminished self-respect.

APPENDIX E:

BOOKS WRITTEN AND PUBLISHED BY DR. BELL:

Publisher, Dorrance Press
643 Smithfield Street, Pittsburg, PA 15222,
Tel: 1-800-788-7654, ISBN 0-8059-3867-2

This is a book of prose and poetry in which Major Chris Bell expresses his impressions of his military experiences and the lessons-learned that came his way. The feelings expressed in these poems have universal application and appeal for most people: whether they are military or civilian, old soldiers or young soldiers, or military wives and mothers. The book's theme and contents clarion the fact that soldiering is a stress filled profession. Further the prose and poetry tell us that the average three-year soldier is bent on following his orders, but he is a thinker too, and he often silently ponders the logic of some of the things he's ordered to do. These poems are brimming with piercing insights that benefit soldiers and the general public and allows the reader to peek into the soldier's mind and sense his thoughts.

"It's a moving tribute to those who experienced Vietnam . . ."
Ronald R. Fogleman, General, USAF Chief of Staff

"What a wonderful way to compile the thoughts and
feelings of your years of military service . . ."
C.C. Krulak, General, Commandant of the US Marine Corps

An excerpt from one of the poems from "Soldiers Do Reason Why..."

Its an Inside Job

Just like a modern-day computer
My mind works hard for me
It faithfully records and stores

All I hear and all I see
It documents my fears and doubts;
It defines my truths from the facts
It tells me what's good and bad
It prompts me on how to act

So I've learned over the years
That what I am or hope to be
Is part of a computer programming
Going on deep inside of me
And that to attain a winning edge
Requires tremendous resolve;
And life's greatest challenge
Is that of the inside job

So feed your computers;
Lots of great self-expectations
Salted with discipline and dedication;
Peppered with work and education,
Mixed with the independent thinking
Uncommon to members of the herd or mob;
Served with a mustard seed of faith . . . ha!
All in all, it'll be an inside job!

This book is out of print, but soon will be revived.

A BOOK THAT DESCRIBES THE LINK BETWEEN CHRISTIANITY, RACE, AND THE PSYCHOLOGICAL BEGINNINGS OF RACISM.

ISBN 1-58500-250X

In this book, Dr. Bell explains how the notion of white superiority is in part subliminally acquired from Christian Trinitarian beliefs. Dr. Bell cites scholarly references as he asserts that the Christian Trinitarian dogma that GOD (the Creator) has a Begotten Son (Jesus), who for centuries has been pictured as a White man is a key subliminal catalyst that promotes a White Superiority Syndrome in both Black and White people.

The book explains how this Trinitarian dogma and its accompanying icons prompt a sense of empowerment and superiority in White people and a sense of inadequacy and inferiority in Black people. Dr. Bell describes the low self-esteem and the negative educational, social, political, and cultural manifestations of Black people who have been blemished by the White Superiority Syndrome. He notes that the black community must stop believing in a "white male savior or Son of God if they are ever to be psychologically free from their sense of racial inferiority, and that this cannot happen until the Black Clergy stops preaching and teaching the Jesus myths (Trinitarian dogma).

SEVERAL AUTHORITIES CITED BY DR. BELL ARE NOTED BELOW.

Dr. Francis Welsing notes (p.166): "Absolutely critical to the White Supremacy system of religious thought was the formation of the image of a White man as the 'Son' of God With this unconscious logic circuit of 'God is a White Man' firmly in place, white domination over non-white people could last for one trillion years."
The Isis Papers; Keys to the Colors

Professor Na'im Akbar states (p.48): "The most obvious problem that comes from the experience of seeing God in an image of somebody other than yourself is that it creates an idea that that image, that person, is superior and you are inferior. Once you have a concept that begins to make you believe that you are not as good as other people, your actions follow your mind. You begin to believe that you have less human potential than one who looks like the image."
Chains and Images of Psychological Slavery

Imam W.D. Mohammed states: "What would happen if people would sit in churches throughout the world for centuries, with the image of an African-American man as Savior of the world before them? What would this do to the minds of the world's children?
Muslim American Journal

BOOK REVIEW QUOTES:

"This is an excellent book for Black Christians and anyone else interested in the far reaching consequences of Black religion. If examined with an open mind, this book could at least positively reform Black Christianity and lessen its negative effects."

Norm R. Allen, Jr.
Executive Director, African American for Humanism, Buffalo, New York

"I share with you the knowledge that racism is deeply related to the structure, both institutional and theological, that create the context for our lives. Your analysis is very consistent with that which the UUA is using to further its anti-racism work."

Reverend William Sinkford
President
Unitarian Universalist Association
Boston, Massachusetts

"Thank you for sharing your book, the Belief Factor and the White Superiority Syndrome. I am delighted to find that other writers have Picked-up this important issue. I commend you on your efforts to persist in the crucial task of bringing a better understanding of these "beliefs" and their impact on our conduct as a people. I will certainly direct people to your book when I invite them to look more closely at the issues of our psychological slavery and the genesis of those chains."

Dr. Na'im Akbar
Executive Director Mind Productions
Tallahassee, Florida

"I want to thank you for sharing your book with me. You have advanced an argument that I haven't seen before and that makes a lot of sense, that is, the Trinitarian formula of belief contains within it an inherent racism and assumption of white superiority, given how the images of Jesus are usually presented. Thank you for your work on this book and for helping me think about old problems in new ways."

Reverend Bruce Marshall, Minister,
Davies Memorial UU Church, Camp Springs, Maryland

THIS BOOK MAY BE ORDERED BY:

a) Contacting the publisher, Authorhouse at www.authorhouse.com, or by calling 888-519-5121. You may identify the book by the author's name or book title or by ISBN#1-58500-250-X

b) Ordering from your nearest bookstore by identifying the book as noted above. The bookstore may order the book by contacting www.amazon.com or www.bn.com or www. borders.com, or the publisher at www.authorhouse.com.

PETITION: NO MORE IDOL GODS FOR BLACK PEOPLE

ISBN# 978-1-4251-7806-2, Price: $19.00

Author explains how and why 'Jesus worship' hurts the black community and emasculates and devalues Black manhood!

THE BLACK CLERGY'S MISGUIDED WORSHIP
LEADERSHIP ISBN# 9781-4251-7806-2 $19.00
By Dr. Christopher C. Bell Jr.

Christopher C. Bell, Jr., Ed.D.

"'Jesus worship' is equivalent to 'white male worship' and is detrimental to the mental and emotional health of black people," argues Dr. Christopher C. Bell Jr. In this book, Dr. Bell cites cogent educational and behavioral reasons to explain why and how the glorification and worship of the ancient, Roman-made, white male, Christian idol, Jesus Christ is not only idolatrous, but how such worship subliminally makes black people complicit in their own psychological oppression. Specifically, Dr. Bell provides information to show that:

The "Jesus Christ" worshipped by black people is the ancient, Roman-made, white male, idol god created by Roman Emperor Constantine and church bishops of the Roman Church at the Nicene Council (CE 325). Jesus worshipping (white male worshipping) reinforces racism in white people and promote psychological self-oppression, self-denigration, and spiritual depression in black people. In addition, Jesus worship subliminally afflicts many black people with an deleterious white superiority syndrome (WSS) that leads to low self-esteem and psychological dissonance; resulting in self-limiting beliefs and aberrant behavior such as; low academic achievement motivation among black adolescents, alienation of black men and women, increased hate toward whites and other blacks, and increased stress related health problems in black males.

Bell argues that to neutralize the above negative effects of "Jesus worship," the black clergy must stop teaching black people to glorify and worship Jesus Christ and begin teaching them a "new Christianity" that espouses WORSHIPPING ONLY GOD the creator and sustainer of life and recognizes Jesus as a human being and prophet. Why? Because this "new Christianity" would remove the unbelievable myths and allegories that make up the Jesus story and make Jesus into a real-life human being and prophet that young black men might relate to with a sense of rationality, human commonality, and self-respect. None of these relationships is possible between today's Jesus myths and young black men.

To order The Black Clergy's Misguided Worship Leadership, ISBN# 9781-251-7806-2: Go to: email: orders @trafford.com, or Tel: 1-888-232-4444. This book is also available at major online book retailers such as Amazon, Borders, and Barnes and Noble.

THE US REVIEW OF BOOKS

The Black Clergy's Misguided Worship Leadership by Christopher C. Bell, Jr. Ed.D
Trafford Publishing
reviewed by Sandra Shwayder Sanchez

"To be black and accept consciously or unconsciously the image of God as a white
man is the highest possible form of self-negation and lack of self respect..."

This book took great courage and deep insight to write. For readers interested in the causes and consequences of racism in our country, as well as for those interested in the history of the development of Christian doctrines and practice, this is an important and enlightening book. The author points out that Jesus the prophet who preached to not perpetuate hostility with anger but to love and forgive, who taught not to hoard but to share wealth, and not to abandon but to care about others, did not, in fact, found the Catholic church.

It was the Roman Emperor Constantine who founded the one universal church of Rome, motivated by a desire to dominate the people of his empire. The author calls this "Constantine certified Christianity" and recommends a new form of Christianity that involves a concept of God that is not restricted to a race and gender specific anthropomorphic entity. Rather he recommends worship of God as the source and sustainer of all life—a universal source of life energy that we all share equally—so that we can all view ourselves and each other with equal respect, regardless of color or gender. He in no way disparages Jesus who would still be honored as a good and gifted teacher.

The author also addresses how this business of worshipping a white male affects relationships between black men and women. Women of all colors will be inspired to consider how the worship of a male figure has affected their lives these past two millennia. For anyone concerned about how religion could and should better motivate everyone to be all that they can be and to make this a better world for all of us, equally, this is a must read—whatever your race, gender or ethnicity.

RECOMMENDED

"Christopher Bell Jr, has written a bold, and courageous book that has been waiting for someone to write . . . No white Jesus can save black folk; we are essentially on our own."

—Molefi Kete Asante, Ph.D., professor,
Department of African American Studies, Temple University

LT. WILLIAMS ON THE COLOR FRONT

ISBN 979-8-88945-025-2
ebook: 979-8-88945-026-9

A NOVEL BY
CHRISTOPHER C. BELL JR.

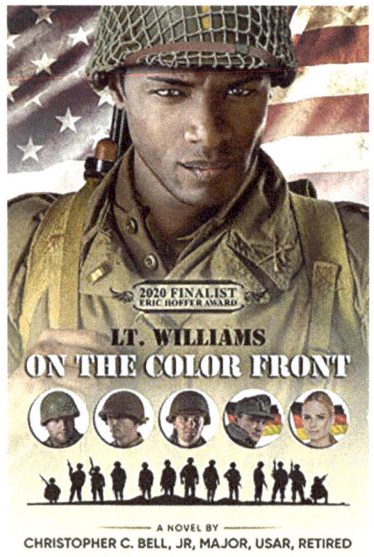

"Lieutenant, I'm neither a member of the NAACP nor of the White Citizens Council," said Colonel Ritter. "But I would have preferred the Department of the army to send me a White lieutenant instead of a Colored one like you."

Now it can be told! In the 1950s, many white U.S. Army officers established a hostile, racial "Color Front" to resist and discourage the assigning of Negro officers to positions of command over white troops.

This novel, Lt. Williams on the Color Front, is an intense, action-filled, coming of age, adventure story of Lt. Neal Williams, a young Colored officer in 1950 who struggles to serve as a platoon leader in an all-white, U.S. Army Infantry regiment in Germany. In the early 1950s, to have a Colored officer in charge of white soldiers could lead to heartburn and conflict; and with Lt. Williams, this is exactly what happens.

This book may be ordered by: 1. Contacting www.Brilliantbooksliterary.com or by calling +1 209 560-0211. You may identify the book by author, title or ISBN#1-4137-6177-1. 2. Ordering from your nearest bookstore and identifying the book as noted above; the bookstore may then order the book by contacting www.amazon.com, or www.bn.com, or www. borders.com.

BEYOND WHITE SUPERIORITY SYNDROME CONDITIONING IN AMERICA

ISBN: 978-1-64674-007-9

ebook: 978-1-64674-009-3

Essays describing the Conscience, Consciousness, and Conscientiousness needed to minimize White Racism

CHRISTOPHER C. BELL JR., Ed.D.

This book is a primer to inspire and inform those persons working to change America's political and social culture from its white supremacy conditioning posture by advancing America's ideals of a culture that truly attempts to build a land of equal opportunity and equal justice for all Americans.

These essays provide information to help both Black and White people to understand how they have been affected by America's White Superiority Syndrome (WSS) conditioning; a conditioning or acculturation that teaches them that a white supremacy culture is good and proper. These essays provide lessons learned by the author that will prompt average people to become more self-aware and better able to identify and resist the various WSS conditioning processes that surround them, and recount some of America's racial hypocrisies and the courage that helped many Americans to challenge them.

PUBLISHER: LITFIRE PUBLISHING LLC publishing@litfirepulishing.com

ABOUT THE AUTHOR: Christopher C. Bell Jr., Ed.D. is a veteran observer of the motivational and behavioral effects of White Superiority Syndrome (WSS) conditioning on Americans, and he has facilitated interracial forum discussions aimed at improving race relations for over 10 years.

This book, BEYOND WHITE SUPERIORITY SYNDROME CONDITIONING IN AMERICA (ISBN) 978-1-64674-0079, is sold at most on-line book dealers such as Amazon, Ebay, B&N, and from the book publisher at order@litfirepublshing

Picture Album

My father, Christopher C. Bell Sr.
c.1968

c. 1938

My birth mother,
A very young Olivia Williams
Date of picture unknown

My birth mother,
Olivia W. Bell, as I
remember her
c. 1944

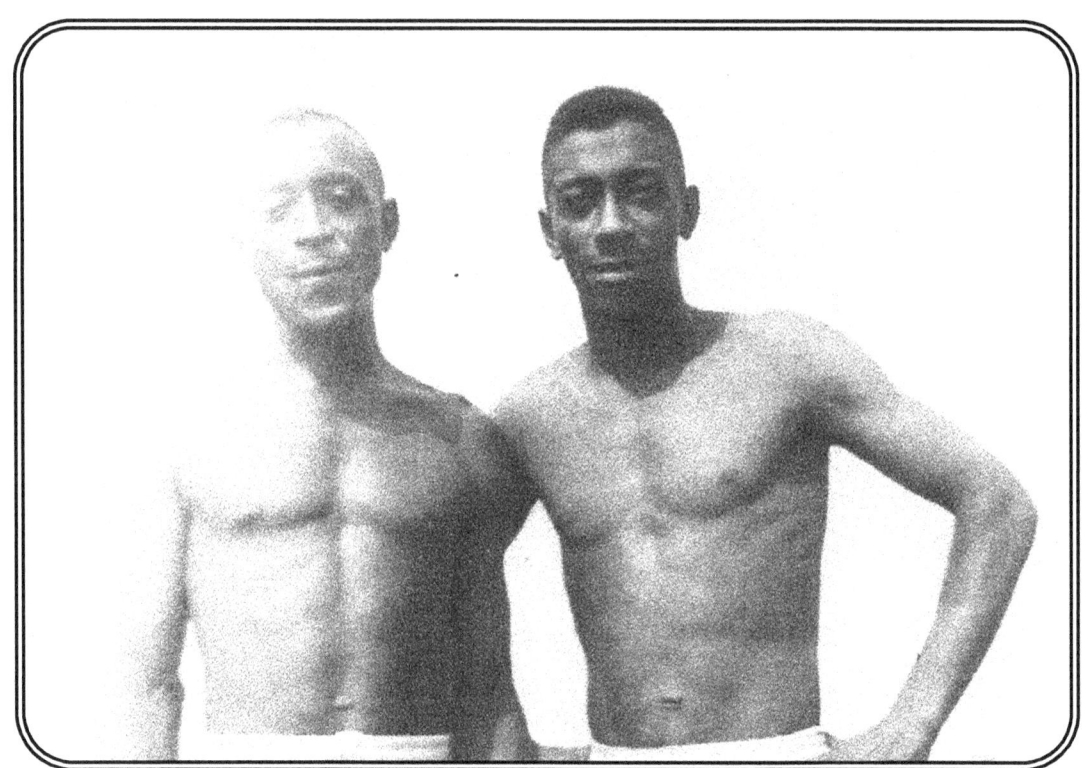

My father and me
c. 1951, Norfolk, Va.

Mama Elsie
Elsie Virginia Armstrong Bell

c.1950

c.2005

Madeline, at age 5 years   Junie (Chris Jr), at age 3 years

Madeline, at age 60 years   Chris Jr, at age 62 years

Student Publication of the Norfolk Division, Virginia State College   Norfolk, Virginia, January, 1952

46-47

School Days

1947-48

Student of the Issue

CHRISTOPHER C. BELL

We, the members of the staff of the Trojan Echo, are pleased to present our "Student of the Issue," Christopher Bell. Mr. Bell resides at 1121 Pike Street, Campostella. He is a member of the Mt. Zion Baptist Church, a life scout, and a junior assistant scoutmaster in Boy Scout Troop No. 74. Mr. Bell is an honor graduate of the February, 1950, graduation class, Booker T. Washington High School, Norfolk.

At the Norfolk Division he is an honor student, a member of the Civic Youth Council, Vice-President of the Student Senate, President of the Debating Society, and is affiliated with many other student organizations.

Mr. Bell is a great community worker. He will be graduated from the Norfolk Division in February, 1952, and plans to attend Virginia State College, Petersburg, to further his education in the field of medicine.

A bright and shining, new army Lieutenant; "Ready for duty" c. 1955

Days as a Lieutenant; South Korea, City of Pusan; c. 1956

In South Vietnam, c. 1967
Carn Rahn Bay Army Depot

As the commanding Officer
of the 596th Petroleum Depot
Company, Fort Lee, Va. c. 1963

Major Bell, preparing for military retirement and civilian challenges

Christopher C. bell Jr.
at 50 years of age

From looking soldierly
to looking scholarly

My Children

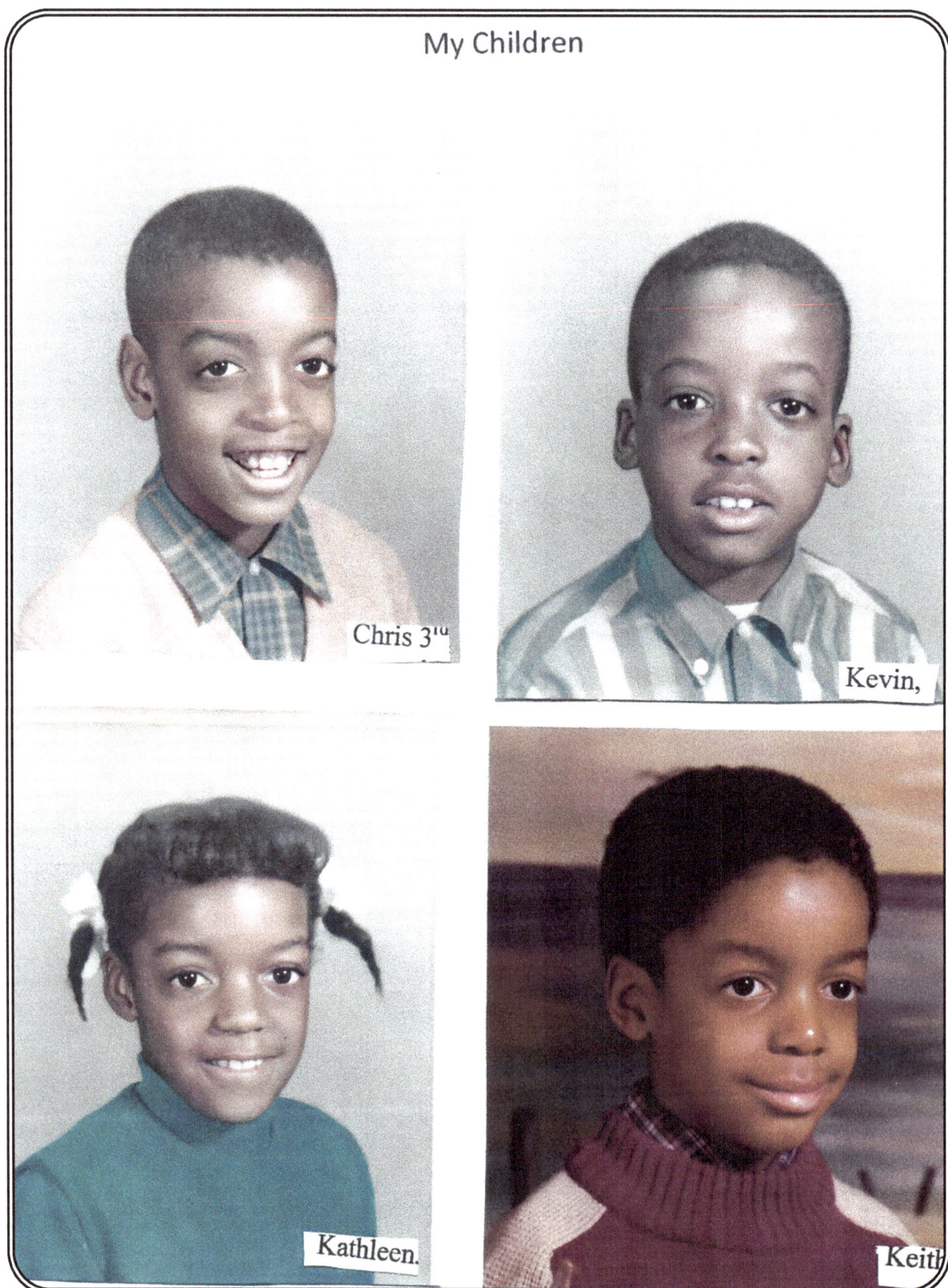

Chris 3ᴿᴰ

Kevin,

Kathleen.

Keith

Mrs. Blanche Jones Bell, my first wife and the mother of my children   c. 1974   and c. 1970

My wife, Mrs. Sadie H. Wiggins Bell

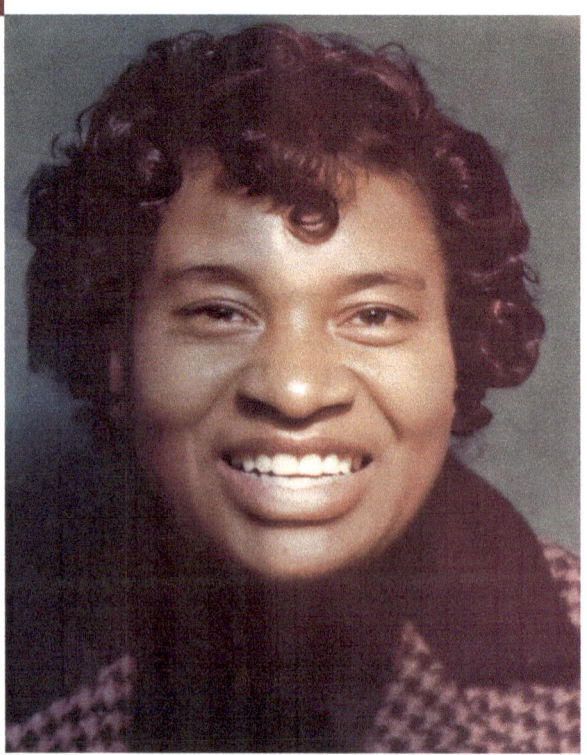

Sadie Wiggins Bell and daughter (my step-daughter) Greta Wiggins-Lewis, President, PGCACDST, at a Delta Sigma Theta Sorority educational function.

The beginning of an Easter morning for Chris, Kathleen, and Kevin

The beginning of Christmas morning for Keith

All my children at my daughter's Kathleen's wedding

Kathleen . . .age: somewhere in her early twenties

My sisters and me, from left to right: Jessie, Marjorie,
Lilie, Author (me), Olivia, and Martha

Granddaddy Henry W. Bell
My father's father, c. 1949

Grandmama Alexina Mullins Bell
My father's mother, c. 1949

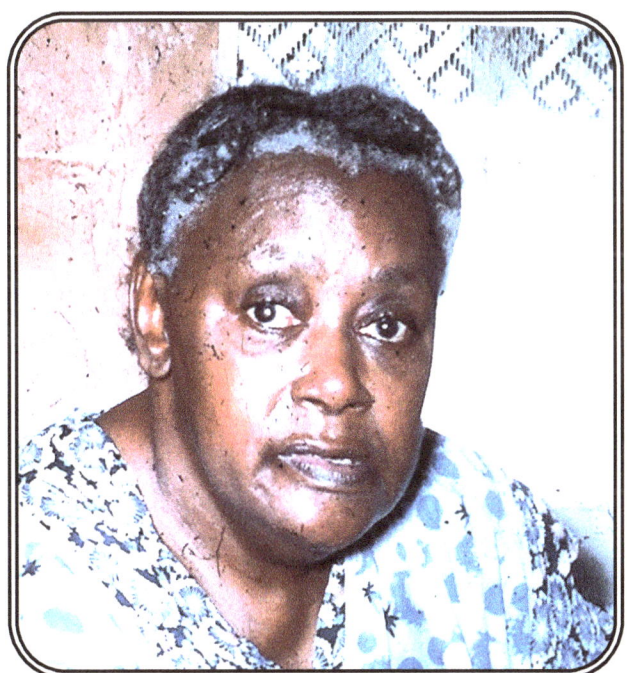

My Children and Grandchildren are
also a part of my Bits and Pieces

My Grandmama Carrie
Bell Williams and me
c. 1952

My Granddaddy Daniel
Williams and me
c. 1952

A family gathering at a C. C. Bell Brotherhood anniversary; at church, Norfolk, Va., c. 1980

Lillie, Olivia, Jessie, Rudell, Marjorie, Chris

All my sisters and me; c. 1993, in Clinton, Md.

Family and friends in smithfield Va., May 2012;
a day after Mama Elsie's funeral

My wife Sadie and me
c. 1986.

Celebration at Andrews Air-force
Base, MD, c. 2003

Hunkered down at reading,
writing, or meditating in my
workshop at home; c. 2005

Personal Coat of Arms
(for Christopher Bell)
designed by M. Paul Lussan
and presentedto the author at
Saint Nazaire, France in 1962

BOSTON UNIVERSITY

THE TRUSTEES UPON THE RECOMMENDATION OF THE FACULTY OF THE

SCHOOL OF EDUCATION

HEREBY CONFER UPON

Christopher Cleophus Bell, Jr., B.S., Ed.M., C.A.S.

THE DEGREE OF

DOCTOR OF EDUCATION

WITH ALL THE HONORS, RIGHTS, PRIVILEGES AND OBLIGATIONS PERTAINING
TO THAT DEGREE.
IN TESTIMONY WHEREOF THIS DIPLOMA IS CONFERRED AT BOSTON,
MASSACHUSETTS, THIS TWENTY-FIRST DAY OF MAY, 1978

Robert A. Dentler
DEAN

John R. Silber
PRESIDENT

Early Freethinkers, Abolitionists, and Unitarians

Early Freethinkers, Abolitionists, and Unitarians and how the three did meet.

Frederick Douglass as portrayed by Dr. Christopher Bell

Speech to Davies Memorial UU Church
Sunday, February 5, 2005

Muslim American Veterans Association, National

20th Anniversary

Outstanding Service Award

Presented to

Christopher Bell
MAVA Co-Founder

In recognition, commemoration and appreciation for your honorable role of service, sacrifice, dedication and commitment in building the Muslim American Veteran's Association, the oldest Islamic established veterans organization in America, into an excellent Veterans Service Organization over the past 20 years (1997 - 2017).

We salute you on your service to Allah through your service to country and humanity.

Presented on this 10th day of November 2017

LYNDON A. BILAL
Commander, MAVA National

TALIB M. SHAREEF, Imam
Vice Commander, MAVA

If I prompt or prod you to think critically about what you worship and how you worship; although such thinking may be uncomfortable or painful for you; I will have done you a favor.

Author and wife Sadie during
cherry-blossom time in Washington D.C.; c.1990

We were somewhere out there, enjoying a piece

Of leisure time

If you will help lead me toward understanding and
transmitting to others the spiritual teachings, the psychological
truths, and the social tools that will combat racial hatred
or enhance and increase social justice, personal
freedom, and human compassion; you will have done me a favor.

Christopher C. Bell Jr.

Dr. Bell

Dedication
of the
QUANTICO MARINE BASE
Islamic Prayer Center

6 June 2006

Thanks for your service to America, *Gordon England* 6-06
Deputy Secretary of Defense

Joshua Dickson   Jordan McBride
William B. Bell Derrick Brown Jr.   Chris Bell Jr. Deidra Bell   Chris Bell 3rd
Aubree Dickson Christe Dickson   Sadie Wiggins-Bell   Kayla McBride
                              Greta Wiggins-Lewis

WHAT ALL AFRICAN AMERICANS SHOULD KNOW ABOUT AFRICAN AMERICAN HUMANISTS

Excerpted from a sermon by Dr. Christopher C. Bell Jr.
Given at the Unitarian Universalist Congregation at Riderwood
Retirement Village, Silver Spring, Maryland
On February 17, 2011

In April 2010, a group of thirty-five (35) American Humanists (AAHs) held its first national conference in Washington, DC. This conference was the first sign of this group's moral courage to go public and to show an open defiance toward Black Christian protocols. The conference was also a harbinger of AAHs future efforts to work to end the "Jesus worshipping" culture within the black community and to direct the community's attention toward humanistic thinking.

WHO WERE THESE AFRICAN AMERICANS HUMANISTS (AAHS) AND WHAT WAS THEIR HUMANISTIC THINKING?

The conference was chaired by Mr. Norman Allen, a black man, who represented the national American Humanist Association (AHA). Most of the participants were not members of the national American Humanist Association (AHA), and one of Mr. Allen's goals was to recruit or encourage participants to become members of the AHA.

Based on the word of mouth testimony of the participants, most of them had been members of a main-line Christian Protestant denominations before becoming a humanist. Some of them were just becoming familiar with the meaning of the word "humanist." Participant's stories varied widely as to how and why they left their Christian denominations and became humanists. But they indicated that now they were glad they left their Christian denominations and that it was helpful to see so many people in one place (the conference) that thought as they did about the problems of dealing with the dogmas and belief requirements of main-line Protestant Christianity.

AAHs, like most humanists, refer to themselves as one of the following names: atheists, agnostics, freethinkers, secularists, deists, mystics, or non-theists. Most of us were not familiar with the American Humanist Manifesto III developed by the AHA.
(For your information this American Humanist Manifesto III is an attachment to this essay. The Manifesto sums up the basic beliefs and aspirations of members of the American Humanistic Association).

The humanistic thinking of AAHs runs parallel with the mode of thinking described in the Humanistic Manifesto III of 2010. In addition, most AAH participants held the following belief: that Humanism is a philosophy of living that is concerned with values, ideals and behaviors that are distinctly human as opposed to values, ideals and behavior that were set up by a superhuman power, and that it is possible for civilized people to create moral codes and ethical rules to live by that would be aspirational toward the uplift, justice, and peace inside their communities and they do not need the aid of a supernatural arbiter.

GENERAL PURPOSES OF THE CONFERENCE:

The purposes of the conference included the following:

A. PROMOTING GROUP SOLIDARITY, mutual support, and fellowship among participants in their efforts to promote their humanistic outlook and outreach. One way of accomplishing this was to listen to each other's most recent lectures or writings and to listen to comments from each other. I was one of several guest speakers. I spoke to the group about my most recent book and explained the connection between what people believed and how people behaved. I explained how Black people's "Jesus worshipping practices" along with other societal and cultural norms had led to black people acquiring a deleterious White Superiority Syndrome (WSS). The gist of my speech is noted in the paragraphs immediately following.

> Christianity offers non-white people a HOPE that living a disciplined and good life here on earth would allow them to enter into a joyful after-life in heaven. However, Christianity's "Jesus worship" is essentially "white male worship" that has a negative effect on the psychological and emotional health of black people. "White male worshipping (Jesus worshipping) is one of the foundational causes (along with poverty, ignorance, and white racism) that often leads to black self-hate and to black people's sense of black racial inferiority. I refer to this state of mind as possessing a White Superiority Syndrome (WSS).

> **This White Superiority Syndrome is the internalized belief and state of mind that white people as a group are inherently genetically and esoterically better human beings than Black people.** This syndrome develops in both black and white people who have been conditioned by the many overt and often subliminal teachings and cultural norms and symbols that celebrate whiteness within America's white superiority and white privileged society. One of the White superiority syndrome conditioning agency among the many, is the Christian church with its Jesus worshipping protocol. As Dr. Akbar (1991) notes in his writings about religion; "**Jesus worshipping requires the Black man to bow down and pray to the likeness (image) of a European white male.**" Such worshipping in conjunction with other American cultural symbols representations of white supremacy, openly and subliminally afflicts many black people with a deleterious feeling of self-hate and a belief in black racial inferiority and white racial superiority; Such worship practices bestows on white people a sense of comfort, control, and white superiority. (Bell, 2010)

> I cited several other black psychologists and educators (Akbar, 1991; Woodson, 1933; Welsing, 1991; Bell, 2001; Sally and Behrn, 1988) who have long stressed the afflictions that Christianity has imposed on the Black community in conjunction with other white superiority symbols and social and economic practices.

B. STRIVING TO MOVE THE BLACK COMMUNITY TOWARD A STATE OF RELIGIOUS LITERACY?

By religious literacy, the AAHs meant to attempt to teach the black community about the history of Christianity and to promote an understanding as to how this religion affected their emotional and psychic development. This religious literacy program would be carried out by individual AAHs. They would formulate and present information bulletins, pamphlets, or undertaking radio and TV discussions, blogs on the world wide web, write books and newspapers articles as well as use other news media to target the black population with an understanding of the effects of Christianity on their thinking.

A Black religious literacy programs would:

1. Lead to black Christians learning to worship only God the Creator and Sustainer of life and thus gain the psychological freedom that will allow black men to develop a sense of authentic self-respect and adult manhood.

2. Result in a cultural awakening in the black community that would change black worship practices; which in turn will lead to changes in White Protestant worship practices, that will in turn eventually lead to a quiet American secular humanistic expansion

C. INSPIRING AND ENCOURAGING HISTORICAL BLACK COLLEGES AND UNIVERSITIES (HBCUS) THEOLOGY AND BLACK STUDY DEPARTMENTS

to alter their curriculum to ensure black would-be preachers or religious teachers are aware of the fantasies, lies, allegories, and fictional stories involved in religious dogmas, and ensure that would-be black preachers are prepared to educate their congregations concerning these fantasies, allegories, and fictional histories as truths.

Why should this matter? AAHs hope that the collegial institutes of study for young black preachers-to-be should add inspiration and encouragement to their student's curriculum that will give these future black preachers **the moral courage** to teach the truth about religion without the added fantasies that now exist in their curricula. Hopefully, these "new" and young black preachers will teach black people to worship only the God of the Creation (which is beyond human imagination) and to regard Jesus Christ as a human being and Jewish prophet.

Most AAHs believe that if HBCU's Theology and Black Studies Departments do not inspire future black preachers to teach the secular history about Christianity, the black community will forever remain in a Holy Helplessness state of mind and remain mired in its own self-oppression and religious gullibility.

D. REQUESTING AND DEMANDING EQUAL "HUMANISM REPRESENTATION" WITH OTHER RELIGIONS AT SO-CALLED INTER-FAITH DISCUSSIONS AND GATHERING.

WHAT DOES IT MATTER?

Humanism representatives who attend and speak at interfaith discussion groups are able to inform the general public about humanism as a respectful alternative to traditional religions, and do so in the same forums in which traditional religions are discussed. This allows the public to become aware of the fact that Humanism is a respected alternative for living a "good" life without having to deal with the fantasies, myths, and dogmas of any one of today's traditional religions.

Are you a Humanist? Whether you're white or non-white (black), now that you know what humanists think and feel, especially the AAHs; do you think and feel as they do?

If you think and feel. that if man is to improve himself, his life or the character of the world in which he lives, he must do it by himself. He cannot count on God to look after him; you may be a humanist.

If you think and feel that "Christianity requires black men to bow down and worship the image of a white male as Lord and Savior, while requiring white men to bow down and worship their own likeness," and that this worship protocol is deleterious to the black man's self -efficacy and sense of authentic first class humanity; you may be a humanist.

If you think and feel that you are one of the following: agnostic, atheist, freethinker, heathen, infidel, naturalist, non-believer, secular, skeptic, rationalist; you may be a humanist.

If you think and feel that religion is man-made wherein men have created gods in their own image or with their basic human characteristics; you may be a humanist.

If you conclude that you identify with at least two of the four choices noted above, you are probably a humanist. But do not be disturbed or discouraged, you are in good company during this your earthly journeying.

References

Akbar, Na'im, <u>Chains and Images of Psychological Slavery</u> New Mind Productions, PO Box 5185, Jersey City, NJ 1991, (p.49, p.61)

Bell, Christopher C., <u>The Belief Factor and the White Superiority Syndrome,</u> Authorhouse, Bloomington, IN, 2001, pp. 29, 30

Sally, Columbus and Behrn, Ronald, <u>What Color is Your God,</u> First Carol Publishing Group, Citadel Press, 1988, p163—167

Welsing, Francis, <u>The Isis Paper; Keys to the Colors,</u> The Third World Press., Chicago Ill, 1991, p.54, p.172

Woodson, Carter G., <u>The Mis-education of the Negro</u>, The Associate Publisher Inc., Washington, DC, 1933, p. 147

HUMANISM AND ITS ASPIRATIONS

Humanist Manifesto III, a successor to the Humanist Manifesto of 1933*

Humanism is a progressive philosophy of life that, without supernaturalism, affirms our ability and responsibility to lead ethical lives of personal fulfillment that aspire to the greater good of humanity.

The lifestance of Humanism—guided by reason, inspired by compassion, and informed by experience— encourages us to live life well and fully. It evolved through the ages and continues to develop through the efforts of thoughtful people who recognize that values and ideals, however carefully wrought, are subject to change as our knowledge and understandings advance.

This document is part of an ongoing effort to manifest in clear and positive terms the conceptual boundaries of Humanism, not what we must believe but a consensus of what we do believe. It is in this sense that we affirm the following:

Knowledge of the world is derived by observation, experimentation, and rational analysis. Humanists find that science is the best method for determining this knowledge as well as for solving problems and developing beneficial technologies. We also recognize the value of new departures in thought, the arts, and inner experience— each subject to analysis by critical intelligence.

Humans are an integral part of nature, the result of unguided evolutionary change. Humanists recognize nature as self-existing. We accept our life as all and enough, distinguishing things as they are from things as we might wish or imagine them to be. We welcome the challenges of the future, and are drawn to and undaunted by the yet to be known.

Ethical values are derived from human need and interest as tested by experience. Humanists ground values in human welfare shaped by human circumstances, interests, and concerns and extended to the global ecosystem and beyond. We are committed to treating each person as having inherent worth and dignity, and to making informed choices in a context of freedom consonant with responsibility.

Life's fulfillment emerges from individual participation in the service of humane ideals. We aim for our fullest possible development and animate our lives with a deep sense of purpose, finding wonder and awe in the joys and beauties of human existence, its challenges and tragedies, and even in the inevitability and finality of death. Humanists rely on the rich heritage of human culture and the lifestance of Humanism to provide comfort in times of want and encouragement in times of plenty.

Humans are social by nature and find meaning in relationships. Humanists long for and strive toward a world of mutual care and concern, free of cruelty and its consequences, where differences are resolved cooperatively without resorting to violence. The joining of individuality with interdependence enriches our lives, encourages us to enrich the lives of others, and inspires hope of attaining peace, justice, and opportunity for all.

Working to benefit society maximizes individual happiness. Progressive cultures have worked to free humanity from the brutalities of mere survival and to reduce suffering, improve society, and develop global community. We seek to minimize the inequities of circumstance and ability, and we support a just distribution of nature's resources and the fruits of human effort so that as many as possible can enjoy a good life.

Humanists are concerned for the well being of all, are committed to diversity, and respect those of differing yet humane views. We work to uphold the equal enjoyment of human rights and civil liberties in an open, secular society and maintain that it is a civic duty to participate in the democratic process and a planetary duty to protect nature's integrity, diversity, and beauty in a secure, sustainable manner.

Thus engaged in the flow of life, we aspire to this vision with the informed conviction that humanity has the ability to progress toward its highest ideals. The responsibility for our lives and the kind of world in which we live is ours and ours alone.

1821 Jefferson Place NW, Washington, DC 20036 // 202.238.9088 // 800.837.3792 // www.americanhumanist.org